The Heart of Legacy

Living a Focused, Faithful, and Fearless Life

DEBBIE SIMMONS

Copyright © 2025 by Debbie Simmons

All Rights Reserved. This book may not be reproduced in whole or in part, in any form or by any means, electronic or mechanical, including photocopying, recording, or by any information storage and retrieval system now known or hereafter invented, except as permitted by U.S. copyright law, without written permission from the publisher.

ISBN: 978-1-964334-08-0 (hardcover)
ISBN: 978-1-964334-07-3 (paperback)
ISBN: 978-1-964334-06-6 (ebook)

Kingdom Business Group, LLC

Table of Contents

Foreword v
Dedication vii

Part 1: My Story

Introduction 3
Chapter 1: Early Life and Influences 9
Chapter 2: Career Beginnings 17
Chapter 3: Family and Personal Challenges ... 28
Chapter 4: Anchor Point's Genesis 48
Chapter 5: Building Anchor Point 53
Chapter 6: Personal Growth Through Your Journey 59
Chapter 7: Looking Ahead 64

Part 2: Lessons Learned

Section 1: Focused

Chapter 8: Know the End Goal 71
Chapter 9: Eliminate Distractions 80
Chapter 10: Next Best Step 90

Section 2: Faithful

Chapter 11: Count the Cost 98
Chapter 12: Believe the Best 103
Chapter 13: Dream Big! 109
Chapter 14: Find Joy in the Journey 115

Section 3: Fearless

Chapter 15: Be Committed and Steadfast 125
Chapter 16: Overcomer—Survive to Thrive. 134
Chapter 17: Resilience and Perseverance 141

Conclusion: Summing Up the Journey. 149
Acknowledgments. 155
Appendix: Anchor Point 157
About the Author 255

Foreword

This book you're about to read is an exploration of legacy—how we leave a lasting impact on our lives, families, and work. I've been given the privilege of introducing it because, well, I've had a front-row seat to seeing its author, my wife, live out these ideas every day.

In her work, she's described as *focused*, *faithful*, and *fearless*. These words capture well the qualities that have guided her through both the calm and the storms, helping her tackle challenges and inspire those around her. Through the years, I've watched her manage our family and lead her non-profit ministry with a steady commitment and a deep-rooted faith. These qualities give her the courage to keep moving forward, even when the path isn't clear or easy.

The truth is, she doesn't shy away from what's difficult. She steps into it—whether that means taking a calculated risk, making a hard choice, or stretching her limits for a purpose she believes in. I've seen firsthand how this mindset has shaped our family's journey and built a legacy of its own, one defined by courage and conviction.

At the heart of all this, though, is her faith. It's a constant, a source of strength and direction that's deeply personal yet shared openly with those around her. It's also the foundation that allows her to give and love without holding back, taking on what she believes in regardless of the risks. I love her, but it is this quality of loving without regard to risk that I also deeply admire.

As you read, I hope her words resonate with you and spark ideas for the legacy you want to create. I'm grateful every day for this journey with her and for the opportunity to support her in the legacy she's building. This book is her invitation to you to do the same.

Her biggest fan,
Scott Simmons

Dedication

To my beloved Nanny,

This book is dedicated to you, my first inspiration for focused, faithful, and fearless living.

You were a constant light in my life, illuminating the beauty of an unshakeable faith and a heart always open to others. Your strength through life's trials taught me how to persevere, and your kindness showed me the power of a warm embrace and a listening ear. You never stopped believing in my dreams, even when they seemed too big or distant. I hope this book reflects the values you instilled in me and honors the incredible legacy you left behind.

Thank you for the laughter, wisdom, and countless ways you shaped me. This is for you, Nanny, with all my love and gratitude.

To Zach, Josh, Nate, and Chris,

How could I not also dedicate this book to you? I have been forever changed because I had the privilege of being your mom. You were perfect children—always loving, never talking back or disobeying—and I (at the time) was a perfect mom.

I held you in my arms as you took your final breaths, and in those sacred moments, you changed me forever. Though your time here was brief, your impact will echo through eternity.

This book is for you—a legacy of the love, strength, and faith you inspired in me. Though I can no longer hold you in my arms, I carry you in my heart every single day. Through these pages, I honor the value and dignity of your lives. Literally, thousands have been impacted for both now and eternity because of you. I cannot wait to be reunited with you in eternity.

Love, Mom

PART 1
My Story

Introduction

"Therefore, my dear brothers and sisters, stand firm. Let nothing move you. Always give yourselves fully to the work of the Lord, because you know that your labor in the Lord is not in vain."

—1 Corinthians 15:58

Welcome to my world. I'm Debbie Simmons, and I've been on a journey for many years striving to become the person God has called me to be. I don't believe I've arrived yet, but every day, I hope I'm becoming more of a reflection of my Father, who loves me deeply. He challenges me to walk in Jesus' footsteps, to grow, and to impact others' lives by pointing them to Him.

God has laid it on my heart to put my life experience into a book. It is nothing short of God's glory, grace, and power that I have anything worth sharing. I hope this book will show how God can use an ordinary person to do great things if we choose to be obedient with each step.

As I thought about summing up what I am sharing, an overarching theme is my belief that we are all building a legacy, day by day, through our actions and choices. This legacy will either impact people for good, bad, or not at all. From an early age, I deeply desired to make a difference and impact people for good. I love the idea that we are living our legacy today and building one that will outlive us.

Further, what can we do to make our legacy God-honoring with lasting kingdom impact in our lives, families, and businesses even after we're gone? This is my story—a glimpse into the marvelous threads God has woven and the journey He's taken me.

As we go through my story, you'll find many highs and lows. But three qualities, in particular, stand out that I think help contribute to building a legacy: focus, faithfulness, and fearlessness. These traits have been a consistent thread in my life, deeply rooted and continually growing. While I'll share my story in greater detail later, let me give you a quick overview of my story and maybe catch a glimpse of those threads.

From a young age, I was determined. I always knew I was precious and deeply loved by my parents. As a little girl, I was a cheerleader mascot for the high school football team, often the center of attention and confident in my ability to achieve things.

This determination led me to become a fearless girl, umpiring baseball games with boys, studying mechanical engineering, and eventually marrying a wonderful man. We wanted to build a family, and though we faced the heartbreak of losing children, we persevered and answered the call of adoption.

God challenged me to build a ministry that could have an eternal impact on thousands of lives—a different path than being an engineer and beyond my volunteering in the church. Through Anchor Point, I've seen lives changed, from the volunteers, donors, and staff to the clients and children whose lives were saved. The ripple effects of our work continue, and I'm grateful for the opportunity to share this journey with you.

Family plays a crucial role in my story. I always wanted children and hoped to get married early, but that didn't happen. We started trying to have children as soon as we married, and infertility became a significant part of our journey. Getting pregnant with quadruplets was another turning point. The boys were born at twenty-six weeks and passed away in my arms. This was a pivotal moment when we chose to trust God with our story.

This loss eventually led us to adoption—first once, then twice, and finally, three times, resulting in our nine adopted children and four boys in heaven. We now have thirteen children. These experiences have shaped how we view life, love, and loss and have influenced the legacy we're building. Each of these moments has impacted how we've made decisions and lived our lives, and I'll explore these themes further as the book unfolds.

You cannot go through losing children and holding them as they pass away without being profoundly impacted. Each of us has a choice as we face hardships: to become bitter or better. Every challenge our family has encountered has given my husband and me the opportunity to grow stronger together, to learn how to weather adversity, to trust that God is writing a good story, and to lean on Him for survival and, ultimately, for thriving. This journey has allowed us to leave a legacy for those who come after us, showing how we walked through our struggles.

As we grew through this season of loss, it became clear that growth in one area spills into others. After the loss of our children, I realized how much eternity mattered and began to reflect on my calling and career. At the time, I was an engineer for Exxon, and while I enjoyed the job, its focus was not impacting lives; it was about tanks, pumps, and gasoline. That was all good, but I felt God encouraging me to do something even more focused on kingdom impact. God continued to challenge me, leading me to leave that career, pursue further education in seminary, and work on church staff. Eventually, He planted a dream in my heart—something far bigger than I could have imagined.

That dream was to build the ministry of Anchor Point, which gives families hope. We come alongside women facing unplanned pregnancies and provide hope for both them and the children they carry. We walk alongside parents through education and resource assistance to help them figure their way on their parenting journey. We lead women through sexual abuse or abortion recovery groups and our trauma reboot series, where they experience freedom for the first time in decades. We partner with families struggling with adopted children from traumatic backgrounds, as well as parents in general, by helping them learn how to love and connect with the child God has blessed them with. God gave us the ability to build this ministry, which has impacted thousands of lives both now and for eternity.

Today, thousands of babies are running around this earth because we have followed God's call, and their moms have hope! Our desire has always been to give people hope, show them that they are not beyond redemption, and offer the support they need to improve their lives. It is our privilege to be the hands and feet of Jesus to these women, families, and children so that we earn the right to share with them about this Jesus we love. When they ask, and they always do, "Why do you do this?" we can say, "Let me tell you about my Jesus."

As I've gone through this journey, and as you will see in this book, I've realized that the foundation of success and legacy-building is found in a relationship with Jesus Christ.

My faith in Him has guided me through this process. It's not about being a superwoman because I am not. I'm just an ordinary woman who has seen God do extraordinary things by seeking to be faithful and obedient and simply taking the next step God has called me to take.

Throughout this journey, and as reflected in this book, God has continued to develop my character so that I might reflect Him more fully to those around me; it is all for His glory. This story is about becoming the person He desires me to be and reflecting His love to others, which allows us to build a legacy. As we journey together through these pages, I pray you will see the hand of God at work and be inspired and challenged to, wherever you are, be a Kingdom player in this world today and in the grander scope of eternity.

To My Lord and Savior, Jesus Christ,

Thank you for being the truest example of focused, faithful, fearless living. You paid the ultimate price for me so that I might be reconciled to God. For this, I am forever changed and forever grateful. You have been my source of strength, purpose, and peace in every season. I know that every gift, every lesson, and every step comes from Your hand. May my life journey honor You and serve as a reflection of Your goodness and grace.

"Every life leaves a footprint in the sand of time, but the deepest and most lasting impressions are made by those who live with passion and purpose."

—Unknown

"He is no fool who gives what he cannot keep to gain what he cannot lose."

—Jim Elliot

"Live, love, laugh, leave a legacy."

—Stephen Covey

"True legacy is how we impact and serve others, reflecting God's love in everything we do."

—Anonymous

CHAPTER 1

Early Life and Influences

"For you created my inmost being; you knit me together in my mother's womb. I praise you because I am fearfully and wonderfully made; your works are wonderful, I know that full well."

—Psalm 139:13–14

Influential Figures

I was blessed to grow up in a wonderful family. My parents both came from large, lower-income, rural families and were among the first in their households to attend college and achieve goals their siblings had not.

Both of my parents were educators and deeply involved in my life. Eventually, they earned their PhDs in education and served as superintendent and assistant superintendent in school districts along the Mississippi Gulf Coast.

My father was my principal for most of my childhood, middle school, and high school years. As a result, I couldn't get away with much; he knew when my games were, what my grades were, and if I was in trouble with a teacher. Thankfully, I was a pretty good kid, so I didn't have much to worry about.

Another influential figure in my life was a woman we called Nanny and her husband, Paw. They were the parents of a high schooler my father coached when he was a football coach. Over time, Nanny "adopted" our family, taking care of my brother and me. We came to see her as a grandmother, which was significant because our biological grandparents had passed away when we were very young. Most of them died before I was born, and the last one passed when I was seven or eight. Nanny and Paw stepped in and lovingly filled the grandparent role for us.

Nanny made an extremely significant impact on my life, whether she realized it or not. She was a woman of deep faith who loved Jesus and loved people. There was never a time when I didn't feel special or that I didn't matter to her. This became especially evident because she struggled with multiple sclerosis (MS) for decades, eventually losing her life to the disease. I had the privilege of walking alongside her through the process of living with this debilitating illness, and I never once saw her without joy.

Even when things were hard, she kept her eyes on Jesus, maintained her joy, and continued to love people. On her worst days, whenever I visited, she was completely focused on me—on my life and how I was doing. I never heard a bitter word from her. She never asked, "Why me?" or complained about her situation. Instead, she lived a life of faith, trusting God, and finding joy even in hardship. This has had a profound impact on me throughout my adult life. I want to be like Nanny. I want to be a person who keeps my eyes on Jesus, who has joy and peace even in difficult times, and who continues to move forward. Nanny's influence was life-changing. You'll hear more stories about her as we go along.

Baptism

One of the most important decisions I made as a child occurred when I was in fifth or sixth grade. My parents would often drop me off at church. They took me to church when I was younger, but as I got older, they would take me to Sunday school and pick me up. They would drop me off at children's choir, then pick me up again. The same went for Vacation Bible School (VBS). Through this, I fell in love with being at church. But that fifth (or sixth) grade year VBS was when I truly realized Jesus loved me, cared for me, and wanted me to have a relationship with Him. I began seeking Him like I never had before, fell in love with Him, and began to understand my need for a Savior and the need for repentance. That moment changed the trajectory of my life.

During that VBS, I decided to follow through with getting baptized. Since my parents had always dropped me off at church, I didn't even think to tell them about the event. It wasn't that they were uninterested in my spiritual journey; I just assumed it wouldn't be a big deal and life would keep moving forward.

The night of the baptism, I had to arrive early. Being a very self-sufficient child at eleven or twelve years old, I packed my extra towel, a change of clothes, and everything I needed. I arrived at the church, got the instructions, and prepared for the baptism. However, the church secretary, who was a friend of my family, realized that my parents weren't planning to attend. She called them, and my mom arrived before the service and said, "We want to be part of this."

I was stubborn and replied, "No, I'm getting baptized tonight, and if you want to see it, you'll have to stay." My father was coaching baseball, and my brother was playing in a game that night, but I stood my ground. I was determined to get baptized that night, and I did. Fortunately, my mom stayed and celebrated my baptism with me.

Looking back on that experience, I now realize I was a very determined, focused, and fearless little girl. If something was important, I would ensure it got done. That same determination has played out throughout my life.

The Ice Cream Incident

When I was about eight, my parents often took my brother and me to the tennis courts. Our job was to pick up tennis balls and try not to argue too much. One night, after picking up the balls without fussing, my dad promised us ice cream. We got in the car and headed to the ice cream shop. My dad brought the cones back to the car. But the flavor he gave me wasn't what I wanted.

He handed my brother his ice cream cone and then asked me, "Do you want this or not?" I responded, "I'm not going to eat that. I want the flavor I asked for."

As you can probably tell from my baptism story, I was a strong-willed child. I told him again that I wanted the flavor I'd originally asked for, and he repeated, "Do you want this or not?" I said no, so he turned around and threw my ice cream away. That night, I didn't get any ice cream, and I was very upset.

As I have reflected on it over the years, the ice cream moment taught me an important lesson: I'm not always the one in control. I have had to recall that lesson and others like it to learn and try to live out the importance of humility and surrender to those in authority over me and, more importantly, to my Lord, Jesus Christ. This means being willing to lay down my way to follow His; this lesson has had a lasting influence on my life.

Life is Precious

Another key area of formation for me as a young girl and follower of Jesus Christ was understanding the preciousness of life. I came to realize early on that there was no reason to end the life of a child during pregnancy, no matter the circumstances. I strongly believe in supporting life and helping young mothers and girls find their way in difficult situations. This belief was deeply rooted within me.

I vividly remember a time in high school when there was a newspaper on the kitchen counter with a story about a mother who had abused her children. I can't recall if it was my mom or dad, but one of them said to me, "If you're going to be pro-life and against abortion, especially for children born into terrible circumstances, then you need to be willing to adopt children like that."

I thought, *Of course, I would.* I was certain that I would step into the gap and adopt children who had been abused, abandoned, or needed love. Little did I know how significant this would become later in my story.

Senior Class President

Another formative incident occurred when I was a junior in high school, and my father was the principal. I decided to run for senior class president. Another girl had also signed up to run, but after I entered the race, she was disqualified due to her conduct grade.

The rumor around the school was that my father had intervened to prevent the other girl from running for senior class president, ensuring I would win. We knew that wasn't true, but it was the talk of the school, making for a difficult and tense couple of months. I wanted so badly to shout that it wasn't the case—that she had been disqualified for her actions, not for anything my father had done.

My mom was frustrated and wanted to complain to the principal—who was my father—so that wasn't an option. She couldn't come to my rescue, and I was left to figure it out on my own.

I remember one morning when I was working in a classroom and overheard students in the hallway talking about me. They were saying hurtful things that weren't true. At that moment, I had to learn to trust that God knew the truth of the situation and that He would take care of it. So, I did; I started trusting Him one step at a time.

When it came time for election speeches, the teachers didn't think it was necessary for me to speak, likely due to the controversy. However, I was determined and said, "No, I'm speaking." I stood before the student body, explained my goals, and asked for their vote.

In the end, I won the election and became senior class president. We had a great senior year, and eventually, the girl who had been disqualified approached me. We sat together, she apologized for everything that had happened, and we became friends again.

This experience impressed upon me that God sees and knows everything. No pain, tear, or struggle goes unnoticed by Him. It doesn't mean that I'll always get the results I want on this side of heaven, but it does mean that He's with me, and I can trust Him to take care of things as He sees fit. I learned to lean into that trust.

That experience was another important lesson in learning to depend on Him—no matter what—and to trust Him with the outcomes.

Through all these moments, God has been weaving a tapestry, laying the foundation for future lessons and experiences in my life. This is the way He works.

"Never be afraid to trust an unknown future to a known God."

—Corrie Ten Boom

"Life is either a daring adventure or nothing at all."

—Helen Keller

"Life isn't about finding yourself. Life is about creating yourself."

—George Bernard Shaw

Make it Personal

1. What are your personal beliefs about faith, and how do they shape your daily decisions?

2. Think about a recent experience where faith played a role. How did you respond, and what did you learn?

3. What does it mean to you to "walk by faith" in both good and challenging times?

4. What step can you take this week to live out the core message of this chapter and inspire others by example?

5. How can embracing this chapter's theme of embracing faith help you make a difference in your community or in someone else's life?

CHAPTER 2

Career Beginnings

"For I know the plans I have for you, declares the Lord, plans to prosper you and not to harm you, plans to give you hope and a future."

—Jeremiah 29:11

Driven From the Start

Even in high school, I was always busy working. I don't know where I got it, but I think I may have picked up some of this from my mother. I was always highly focused on reaching my goals and objectives.

In high school, I was in the band, served as senior class president, played volleyball, basketball, and softball, and participated in student council. I did it all while maintaining excellent grades and graduating with honors.

I've always been a focused and driven person who can achieve the goals I set for myself. I started babysitting as a young kid because it was easy money, and I loved playing with children. God gave me a heart for kids, so babysitting was fun and enjoyable.

Later, I found myself working in jobs dominated by men. My father was a baseball umpire, and we grew up playing softball and baseball. He was my coach. During Little League, they needed someone to work in the score booth, and they paid pretty well. My father taught me how to keep score, which I did during summers. I learned the rules of baseball and all the ins and outs of the game.

As I got older, I noticed that some of my male friends were umpiring games and making more money than I was in the booth. Interestingly, I knew the rules better than they did, as they would often turn around during games and ask me questions. I realized that I knew more than they did, yet they were making double what I was. That didn't sit well with me; I wanted to be an umpire.

When I told my father that I wanted to umpire, he said, "No, girls don't do that." But I persisted. After a few weeks, I brought it up again, and he still said no. Eventually, the lead umpire suggested I consider umpiring, which gave me the confidence to ask again. I told my father, "Dad, I'm going to umpire. You have to help me."

He finally relented but refused to let me go behind home plate during my first year. I had to umpire everything with him. This was his way of protecting his little girl, making sure I knew what I was doing while still helping me achieve my goal, even though he wasn't entirely sure it was a good idea.

So, we began our journey of umpiring together. I knew I was determined and would figure this out. However, I also understood that I was entering a male-dominated world, so I needed to be sure I knew what I was talking about and doing.

I studied the baseball rule book thoroughly, but my dad only allowed me to umpire in the field. I only umpired the bases during that first year, while my dad always called each game with me behind the plate. At the end of the season, they were looking for umpires for the league playoffs, and they called my dad. After receiving the call, my dad got off the phone and said, "See, they called the best."

I shrugged it off, thinking, *Okay, whatever; it's just my first year.* Thirty minutes later, I received a call inviting me to umpire the playoffs with my dad. I hung up and told my dad, "Hey, look, they do call the best."

My dad allowed me to start calling behind the plate the following year. I ended up umpiring up to the junior college level, continuing for several years into my marriage. Umpiring taught me valuable lessons; chief among them was the importance of remaining cool and calm under pressure. Whether it was angry coaches in my face or high school boys questioning my knowledge because I was a woman, I learned to stay composed and trust my abilities.

This experience, my first real job, helped me develop confidence, resilience, and the ability to handle difficult situations without being rattled. These lessons have served me well in life.

In addition to umpiring, I also worked as a lifeguard, which came with the responsibility of overseeing people's safety. Managing the pool and ensuring the safety of swimmers taught me further lessons in responsibility and leadership.

I did all these jobs simultaneously—umpiring, cleaning dorm rooms, and babysitting—anything I could to reach my goals, expand my skills, make money, and pursue the things I wanted to do or felt God was leading me to do.

College, Exxon, and More Male-Dominated Fields

In college, I majored in mechanical engineering, which was another male-dominated field at the time. I ultimately became president of the American Society of Mechanical

Engineers, graduated, co-opted with DuPont, and had many great experiences.

These experiences led me to accept a job at Exxon as a plant engineer, where I handled all maintenance and construction at terminal facilities to ensure gasoline was available at the pumps. This role stretched me, as it was a male-dominated world, but it also taught me how to work with large groups of people to accomplish big projects. I learned how to break down the steps needed to achieve a goal and how to get people on board to make it happen.

I truly enjoyed my work as an engineer; it was fun and pushed me to grow and learn new things. I discovered that I preferred hands-on work over theory and that I was a people person who wanted to make a difference. One key thing I learned was that I loved project management but did not enjoy bureaucracy. I loved being in the field, working with plant operators, and building and developing projects.

Seminary? No Way!

However, over time, God made it clear that what I was doing would no longer bring me satisfaction, and this holy discontent was leading me in a different direction. One day, He put the thought in my head that maybe I needed to go to seminary to be trained so I could have more Kingdom impact. At that time, I had been teaching children's choir at the church, and that had eternal impact. But I felt God calling me to make a larger commitment and make an eternal difference in people's lives vocationally.

Initially, I thought it was the craziest idea I had ever heard and dismissed it. I knew myself and that we were part of a Baptist church, and at that time, there weren't many women serving as pastors or key leaders. I thought, *God, you've got the wrong person.* However, He continued to nudge me, challenging me to be open to this path. I resisted for about two years.

One night, while my husband and I were outside stargazing—something I don't do very well, as I struggle to sit still—he said out of the blue, "I think you need to pursue seminary."

I was shocked. "What? Are you serious?" I asked.

He responded, "Yes."

I couldn't believe it, but he was adamant.

I finally said, "Okay, fine. I'll look into it."

I began researching. The only seminaries I knew of were in Fort Worth and New Orleans, but we lived in Houston. I wasn't sure how it would work. I called the seminary in Fort Worth and spoke to someone in the registrar's office, asking for a catalog to review the courses.

The woman on the phone offered to send me an application along with the catalog, but I insisted, "No, I don't need the application—just the catalog." I didn't think I was qualified for this. She said, "No problem, I'll send both." Despite my protests, she sent the application anyway.

When I received the materials and started reading the catalog, I realized I could handle the coursework. Seminary was within my reach. Reluctantly, I decided to fill out the application. I had been slow to obey, but as I've grown older, I've learned that obedience is essential.

Completing the application meant I had to speak with my pastor and tell him I believed I was being called to ministry, even though I wasn't entirely sure of it myself. When I met with him and shared my thoughts, he affirmed everything. I was still in disbelief, but he reassured me that this was real.

He then explained, "We'll need to have a business meeting, and you'll need to present this to the church. They'll have to agree to send you to seminary."

I couldn't believe I had to stand in front of the church body and tell them that I thought I was called into ministry, especially when I was still wrestling with whether I believed it myself. At the business meeting, my pastor had me stand before the congregation and explain that I believed God was calling me to ministry and that I needed to pursue formal training. The entire time, I was thinking, *What am I doing?*

To my surprise, the congregation agreed, and they even licensed me and ultimately ordained me into ministry, which is quite remarkable in a Baptist church. I sent in my seminary application.

On the application, there was a section for additional information, so I decided to list every sin I could think of that I had committed, hoping they would turn me away. However, to my amazement, I was accepted.

This required a bold step for Scott and me. We learned that I could attend school at a branch campus in Houston, which was a relief, but going to school meant I would need to leave my job at Exxon. Scott was still a full-time graduate student, not close to finishing his doctoral work, and would need to find a job to support us.

I gathered a group of close friends and asked them to pray. Specifically, I asked them to pray that if this was truly God's will, He would provide Scott with a job that would fall directly into his lap—one that he would love, pay a certain amount, and that they'd be eager for him to take. Within two weeks, Scott, who isn't the planner in our family, happened to stop by the placement office and see a job posting that interested him. He had interviews and was offered a job at NASA, where he still works today and absolutely loves his job. Although the job didn't quite meet the salary we had prayed for, we trusted God to provide.

So, within a month of each other, Scott began his career at NASA, and I left engineering to pursue ministry. My early faith walk and trusting God, even when we didn't know the outcome, were pivotal in building my faith and obedience. It helped me learn to say yes more quickly as I continued down this new direction.

From there, God led me on a journey. My career path has not been a straight line; it zigzags all over the place. I went from being an engineer to earning a Master's in Christian Education to working on a church staff. Along the way, I learned that working on church staff isn't always easy. You often see the messy side of Christian life, but it's still good and worth pursuing.

We eventually moved back to Houston. I thought God would place me in a church again, but He didn't. That was a difficult realization. By that time, I had also earned a master's in organizational management, which allowed me to work in an organization teaching car salespeople how to sell. That experience taught me valuable skills in asking questions, painting a picture of the future for people, and giving them hope—not just with their vehicle but in life.

Prison Fellowship and More Unexpected Turns

Later, I took a position with Prison Fellowship, founded by Chuck Colson, where I led prison ministry across four states. That experience was incredibly valuable. Chuck Colson was President Richard Nixon's White House counsel and hatchet man. He served time for his Watergate-related crime. Chuck accepted Jesus as his Lord and Savior in 1973 before heading to prison. After his incarceration, Chuck felt led by God to never forget those he left behind in the prison. Under God's direction, he built Prison Fellowship into the world's largest family of prison ministries. While I had the honor of working at Prison Fellowship, I watched him successfully transition out of leadership at Prison Fellowship and focus on writing, leaving behind a ministry that still thrives today. Being part of that was highly influential for me.

I also learned that many people in prison are often freer than those of us outside because they've learned to surrender and trust God, even though they may spend the rest of their lives behind bars. That gave me a new perspective on my Christian walk and how I could remain faithful.

While I was working with Prison Fellowship, I began to sense that God was calling me to do something bigger—to start Anchor Point. My initial response was, *I'm not doing it.* I was already in full-time ministry and raising seven adopted children, which alone felt like a full-time ministry. Starting something new would cost a lot of money, and I told God, *You've got the wrong person. I'm already doing enough. How can you ask more of me?*

I had a bit of a pity party, and that thought lingered for about a year. God kept bringing it back to my mind, but I refused to budge. Then, one of the most painful experiences of my life happened. My job at Prison Fellowship was abruptly removed in the span of a week due to miscommunication and misunderstanding. In the end, it was better for me to walk away, wish the ministry success, and leave them set up for the future.

The process was extremely painful for me, and it was a real disappointment. However, as I walked through that challenge, I aimed to ensure my children learned how to handle difficult situations. My husband and I discussed it and decided to plan a "what's next" party. The purpose of this party was to focus on where God was working and the doors He was opening, even as another door was closing. We wanted to choose not to be bitter but to be better, to wish the organization well, and to trust that if any truth needed to come out, it would do so in time. I didn't need to worry about that—God had me.

The Heart of Legacy

"Debbie is one of the most effective people we have had in Prison Fellowship. She is great at building relationships and is a poised and confident leader. She puts everything she has—and that's a lot—into her work. She is a very talented, gifted leader. Count me among her fans and supporters."

—Chuck Colson
Founder, Prison Fellowship

As I walked through this experience, God placed a thought in my mind: *Now that all your time is free, is there any reason you can't start Anchor Point?*

I responded, *Okay, God, I'll do it. I'll do whatever You ask.*

The pain of that transition made me more willing to surrender when God opened that door again. From that moment of surrender and humility, I've never looked back. While I'm not always humble and fight it at times, I haven't resisted God as long as I did during that season or when I resisted the call to seminary. I've seen His faithfulness too many times.

Now, my faith muscle is much stronger. Most of the time, when I feel God prompting me, I say, "Yes, God, I'll do it, whatever You want." Sometimes, I'm even brave enough to ask, "Okay, God, what do You want me to do next? Just show me, and I'll follow."

This faith muscle is something I wouldn't have developed without these experiences. I am so grateful.

"Faith never knows where it is being led, but it loves and knows the One who is leading."

—Oswald Chambers

"Will God ever ask you to do something you are not able to do? The answer is yes—all the time! It must be that way, for God's glory and kingdom. If we function according to our ability alone, we get the glory; if we function according to the power of the Spirit within us, God gets the glory."

—Henry Blackaby

"Do not go where the path may lead, go instead where there is no path and leave a trail."

—Ralph Waldo Emerson

Make it Personal

1. Describe a situation where you struggled with timing or patience. How did that impact your trust in God?

2. How do you view seasons of waiting in your life, and what have they taught you about resilience?

3. How can you be more open to God's timing rather than pushing for your own?

4. What step can you take this week to live out the core message of this chapter and inspire others by example?

5. How can embracing this chapter's theme of trusting God's timing help you make a difference in your community or in someone else's life?

CHAPTER 3

Family and Personal Challenges

"But He said to me, 'My grace is sufficient for you, for my power is made perfect in weakness.' Therefore I will boast all the more gladly about my weaknesses, so that Christ's power may rest on me."

—2 Corinthians 12:9

Hidden Struggles and Radical Love

When Scott and I were in college at Mississippi State, I was eager to get married while we were still in school so we could start trying to have children. I had this vision of being an ideal young grandmother, which likely stemmed from the fact that my grandparents had mostly passed away before I was born. Watching Nanny suffer for years with multiple sclerosis only reinforced my desire to be active and involved with my future grandchildren.

I thought that if I found the man I was going to marry, we should get married as soon as possible and start having kids. As you know from my story, I'm determined, so I did my best to convince Scott to marry me early. However, he insisted we finish school first, so I had to wait.

Once we graduated, got married, and moved to Houston, we quickly started trying to get pregnant. Unfortunately, we struggled with infertility due to polycystic ovarian disease (PCOD) and other issues. We began a journey of fertility treatments to see if we could conceive.

Infertility is an incredibly challenging process, both physically and emotionally. It made me question my identity. Here I was, with this strong desire to be a young grandmother and a heart full of love for children, and yet I couldn't even get pregnant. It seemed like everyone around me was having babies. Every Sunday school class revolved around discussions of pregnancies and due dates, and I couldn't help but feel left out.

That experience opened my eyes to the hidden struggles others might be going through. It taught me to be more gracious and understanding, realizing that people might be facing challenges they aren't openly sharing.

Scott and I continued with fertility treatments, and we were able to participate in a study at Baylor College of Medicine for a new fertility drug. Unbeknownst to us at the time, we were given the actual drug, not the placebo. We had three tries to conceive.

The first attempt was unsuccessful, and I remember being devastated. When I realized it hadn't worked, I went home, threw myself on the bed, and felt utterly defeated. I questioned my worth as a woman, a potential mother, and a spouse. It felt like my dream of becoming a mother was slipping away, and I couldn't find a way to make it happen.

When Scott came home and saw how upset I was, he asked, "What's wrong?"

I responded, "I'm not pregnant. Life is over."

Being the good man he is, Scott took me out to dinner to comfort me. However, as we sat there, I grabbed the edge of the table and said, "You will not fix me tonight. I will be miserable, moody, and fussy. Tomorrow, I'll be okay, but tonight, I'm staying in this pain."

Scott realized I wasn't in a place to be "fixed" at that moment, so he graciously asked, "What would you like to talk about?" We made it through the evening, and I learned an important lesson: it's okay to sit in your pain for a while, but it's also important not to stay there permanently.

The next day, I got up, faced life again, and we tried for a second time, but that attempt was unsuccessful as well. Finally, on the third try, we received the news we had been waiting for—we were pregnant.

That day, we had two doctor's appointments: one with the fertility specialist and another with our OB-GYN. At both appointments, about two hours apart, I had ultrasounds—one abdominal and one vaginal. To our surprise and delight, both ultrasounds revealed that we were having twins! I was thrilled because I had always wanted four children, and having two at once would make the process faster. I was still focused on being a young grandmother.

Scott and I were overjoyed. We left the doctor's office with renewed hope and excitement as we began planning for the family we were building. At the time, I was working at Exxon as the breadwinner while Scott was still in graduate school.

We continued our journey. I was about five weeks along, and we were still trying to figure out how to manage with me as the sole breadwinner at the time. However, we became comfortable with the idea that we would find a way to make it work. Life went on, and so did the pregnancy.

During the holidays, we went home to share the news with our families. We told them we were pregnant with twins, and they were all super excited. I was already starting to feel tired, but everyone was looking forward to what was ahead.

After the holidays, we returned to Houston. One day, Scott dropped me off at the Exxon building for work, and as I was riding up the elevator, I suddenly started bleeding. I was almost thirteen weeks along, just shy of finishing the first trimester, which is the most critical time for miscarriages.

I remained calm outwardly, but inside, I was panicking. Nobody at the office knew what was going on, and since this was before the age of widespread cell phones, it was hard to get ahold of Scott. I went up to my office and informed my boss, who was leaving for a trip, that I would need to talk to him when he returned. He didn't even know I was pregnant.

Then, I started calling my new doctor, whom I hadn't seen yet due to my recent change in insurance. They told me to go to the emergency room. I managed to find my car, drove myself to the ER, and kept trying to reach Scott, but I couldn't get ahold of him.

When I finally arrived at the emergency room, they told me to sit and wait. Throughout infertility and our pregnancy journey, I learned it's always "hurry up and wait." I sat there calmly, realizing I had no control over the situation. I prayed for the babies, trusting God with whatever happened next.

Eventually, they brought me back and listened for a heartbeat. They could pick up one, though they weren't sure if they were hearing one or two heartbeats. For some reason, they didn't do an ultrasound, but they said the bleeding had stopped. They told me it looked like I was attempting to miscarry but that I should go home, rest over the weekend, and contact my OB-GYN.

By then, Scott had caught up with me, and we went home to wait through the weekend. The problem was that with the new insurance plan, I didn't know any of the doctors. I was immediately referred to a high-risk OB-GYN, both because I was carrying twins and because of the emergency room visit.

That Monday, Scott and I went to the high-risk OB-GYN's office. As we sat in the waiting room, I joked, "Watch, they're going to tell us we're having three instead of two." Scott and I both laughed it off, but when we went in for the ultrasound, we were in for a surprise.

The ultrasound tech was very kind. It was a high-risk facility, so the room was large, with a big TV screen displaying the ultrasound images. As soon as the probe touched my stomach, I could tell there were three sacs. The tech said, "Oh, there are three," and I responded, "Yes, I see."

Sitting across the room, Scott put his head in his hands and muttered, "I don't know what we're going to do." After a while, the tech continued taking measurements and said, "Let's get a picture of all three for you, Mom."

As she moved the wand around, I suddenly noticed something: there were four. I said, "Oh, there are four." Then, I told her, "This is already a high-risk pregnancy, so let's not bother looking for a fifth. Four is plenty."

The tech, clearly surprised—this was probably her first time scanning quads—took more measurements and said, "I think I need to get the doctor."

By this point, Scott was pacing back and forth across the room, anxious and overwhelmed. Remember, I was the breadwinner, and this was a lot to process. The doctor came in, hugged me, and assured us that she would help us navigate this journey. She confirmed that there were indeed four babies and explained I had likely been attempting to miscarry because I hadn't been eating or drinking enough to support four children. She told us that in about two weeks, I would likely be put on bed rest for the remainder of the pregnancy and that things were going to change dramatically. She also informed us that we needed to see a specialist to discuss the option of selectively reducing (another word for aborting) the number of babies we were carrying.

At that moment, I was in shock—not panicking but overwhelmed by the gravity of the situation, being put on bed rest, being the breadwinner, and now carrying quadruplets. How in the world would we navigate this? I wasn't sure. I knew that God loves babies, and I trusted that He had a plan. However, so many unknowns were swirling in my mind and in my husband's, too.

After all the ultrasounds and the realization that we were expecting four babies, Scott dropped me back off at work. My boss wasn't there, but his boss was, so I asked to speak with him. I said, "I realize you don't know this, but I thought I was pregnant with twins. It turns out I'm pregnant with quadruplets. The doctor told me that within two or three weeks, I may have to go on bed rest for the remainder of the pregnancy. I need to figure out what accommodations Exxon can make so I can continue working as long as possible."

He looked at me, shocked—who expects someone to be pregnant with four babies? But he was gracious, kind, and quick to help. Exxon made accommodations allowing me to work longer, partly from home and partly in the office, where they even set up a recliner. They were incredibly supportive during that time.

By the time I got home that night, I called my parents. There haven't been many times in my life when I've lost control, but when I talked to my mom, I broke down. I said, "Mom, I'm pregnant with four. How am I going to do this? This is overwhelming. I don't know what I'm going to do." My mind raced with questions: *How will we afford this? How will my car fit four car seats? How will I take care of four kids? I'm the breadwinner—how can I afford all the diapers? How will we pay for college? What if they're all girls—how will we afford four weddings?*

My mom stopped me and said, "Why don't you focus on today, and we'll figure out the rest as it comes?"

At that moment, my body relaxed. I realized I didn't have to worry about tomorrow. I just had to focus on today—resting, taking care of myself, and figuring out the next step. That advice from my mom was a blessing she probably doesn't even realize she gave me.

Then, my dad got on the phone. He's a man of few words, but what he said meant everything to me: "Daddy's going to take care of you." As a grown woman, hearing those words from my dad brought me so much comfort. It was a reminder that my earthly father would take care of me and that my heavenly Father would, too. I could trust God to take care of me as I fully relied on Him.

That conversation marked the start of a new faith journey for us. Every day of the pregnancy required us to focus on just that day, figuring out how to survive and make it through, one day at a time. We visited with our pastor, knowing that we didn't have much family support nearby and would need help. On our way into the meeting, the church secretary told Scott, "God wouldn't put you in this situation if He didn't know you could handle it."

We didn't know what our journey would look like, but we believed that God would take care of us, and our pastor prayed with us as we began this new chapter.

The pregnancy itself was an adventure. I had to drink gallons of water daily and learn to care for myself and the babies. We eventually met with a doctor to discuss the possibility of selective reduction, which involves ending the lives of one or more babies to increase the survival chances of the others. This doctor was renowned for his skill in performing these procedures, but that only made the conversation more difficult.

He spent about three hours with us explaining the process. He recommended reducing the number of babies from four to two to increase the likelihood of a successful pregnancy. He walked us through the pros and cons of this approach, with the goal of carrying the babies to thirty to thirty-four weeks. He also discussed the option of continuing to carry all four, explaining what that might look like, including the risks, the need for bed rest, and other factors.

Ultimately, the doctor said that, in either case, there was a fifty-fifty chance that the babies would survive and that I would make it through the pregnancy. As someone deeply committed to life, I had always believed that the life I carried was given to me by God, and it wasn't my right or choice to end that life. I knew going into the appointment that I wouldn't opt for selective reduction, but our doctor insisted we consult with the specialist, so we did.

During the appointment, I asked the specialist out of curiosity, "If you choose to selectively reduce, how do you decide which child to eliminate?"

He responded, "Whichever one is easiest to reach with the needle."

I was stunned. "But what if that's the healthiest child?" I asked. "What happens then?"

He explained, "That child would die in the womb, and when you give birth, you will pass all of the children."

I knew at that moment that I could never go through with it. I entered the appointment, certain I wouldn't do it and left even more resolved. After the appointment, I told my mom that we had decided not to selectively reduce and to carry all the babies. She wasn't happy with our decision. If she had been in our situation, she probably would have chosen to reduce the number of babies to increase the chances of survival. She left Texas upset with us, but by the time she returned to Mississippi, she called to apologize and became an incredibly supportive grandmother.

That experience opened my eyes to how easily young women can be pressured by family members to make life-altering decisions, including ending a pregnancy. It was a formative lesson for me during that time.

We decided to carry all the babies, and though there were many highs and lows, it was also an exciting time. As we reached twenty-three weeks, I grew larger and moved around less. Our goal was to make it to thirty weeks, and we were getting close. We decided to tour the hospital, knowing that I wouldn't be able to move around much soon.

We headed to Hermann Hospital, about a thirty-minute drive from our house in Houston. Traffic was heavy on I-45, and we had to stop abruptly. Unfortunately, the car behind us didn't stop in time and hit us. The impact wasn't severe, and our car was still drivable, but I remember thinking, *I don't feel very good.*

We documented everything, and after the police issued a ticket to the other driver, I told Scott, "I don't feel well. If we're going to the hospital, we should go now because I might not want to come back after this."

When we arrived at the hospital, I felt even worse, so I asked the nurse to put me on a monitor to check for contractions. I wasn't feeling anything specific, just an overall sense of not being well. The nurse agreed, and it turned out I was having contractions two minutes apart and trying to go into labor. They hydrated me, stabilized me, and kept me overnight before sending me home.

Two weeks later, I woke up one morning to find that my water had broken. At first, I didn't realize what had happened, but once I figured it out, I told Scott, "We need to call the doctor. I bet they're going to put me in the hospital and not let me out."

I packed my things, and we headed to the doctor's office. Once again, we found ourselves hurrying up and waiting. After a long wait, they confirmed via ultrasound that one of the sacs had ruptured, and I needed to be admitted to the hospital.

Knowing I'd be staying for a while, I convinced Scott to stop for a big hamburger before we went to the hospital; I knew I'd be stuck eating hospital food from then on.

Once we arrived, they didn't have a room ready for me, so they put me in a recently painted room that smelled awful. I hadn't eaten enough, and I was feeling hungry and exhausted. I remember asking Scott to stay with me for the first night. I knew he'd have to go to work the next day, but I needed him to stay that night.

While Scott went home to gather more things, I watched a movie on TV about a family with quadruplets. The father was trying all kinds of funny tricks to feed the babies, using a stick to rock all their car seats at once and attaching bottles to the stick so he could feed them simultaneously. Watching that scene, I felt overwhelmed. I was exhausted, trapped in bed, and beginning to panic.

Just then, my pastor walked in, having somehow found out I was there. He prayed for me, which brought me some comfort. My mom called and told me she and my dad would start driving early the next morning to be with me.

Scott and I made it through that first night. We played cards, and I tried to keep my mind off everything. The next morning, I woke up in pain. One of the babies was either sticking a hand or foot through my stitched cervix. It was time. One of the babies was ready to come.

The doctors came in, checked me, and prepped me for surgery to remove the stitches from my cervix. Afterward, they waited to see what would happen. My mom and dad arrived in town, which meant a lot to me. Sometimes, a girl just needs her mom and dad. Scott was there, of course, but having my parents there felt different, more comforting.

Not long after, Zach was born. I was twenty-six weeks along. His lungs weren't developed enough, so they immediately handed him to me. He couldn't breathe and essentially suffocated in my arms, but he took my finger in his tiny hand and held on tightly. At that moment, I felt nothing but pure love and joy. Scott and I cherished that brief time with him before he went to be with Jesus.

My parents, who had once told me that if I was pro-life, I needed to be willing to adopt, held their grandchild, born at twenty-six weeks—perhaps a child they would have considered aborting if they had been in my shoes. The gravity of holding their grandchild, I believe, changed my mom's perspective over the years.

After Zach passed, the question became whether my body could handle carrying the other three babies or whether I would become too sick, forcing us to induce. My fever began to spike to 103 or 104 degrees, and I was rapidly deteriorating. The doctors decided to induce the other three babies; Josh, Nate, and Chris were born close together. Like Zach, they were too young to survive, and I held them as they passed away.

April 1, 1995, became both a birthday and the day I lost four children. It was an incredibly hard day. However, even amidst the hardship and heartbreak, I felt an overwhelming sense of peace and calm. I have rarely, if ever, felt God's presence as strongly as I did then. He was there with Scott and me through every step. No part of the process was neglected or overlooked by Him.

Although losing my boys was devastating, God's hand was evident throughout the entire experience. Simple things fell into place, like when we decided to mail a birth and death announcement to let family and friends know what had happened so they wouldn't be caught off guard. We had memorial services and a funeral. My Nanny even gave me burial plots for the boys, where Scott and I could eventually be buried with them. It's not something you typically plan for, but God took care of everything.

The funeral home in Houston handled all the arrangements at no cost because it was an infant loss. My former church music pastor, who worked at the funeral home in Mississippi, took care of the burial. God's provision was clear in so many ways.

That night, after the boys were born, I lay in the hospital bed, and Scott climbed into bed with me to hold me. I remember clearly feeling like I had a choice: I could become bitter or better. I told God, "I don't know how to go on. I want to scream *Why!* over and over again, but I don't know how to survive this. However, I trust You. I will put a stake in the ground and know that You are for me, not against me. You know my heart, love for children, and desire to be a young grandmother. You can make something good come from all of this, and I will trust You."

From then on, I leaned heavily into trusting Him, even when I didn't know how. Sometimes, I could only go a few minutes before I had to remind myself to trust Him again. Other times, I made it through an hour or even a day. Slowly, I found my way forward. After a significant loss like this, you go through a minimum of a whole year of grief, learning what your new normal looks like. Mother's Day, Father's Day, birthdays, Christmas—everything changes. We had to learn how to navigate this new normal.

Grief and Hope

As we moved through that first year, I asked God to show me how to survive. He did step by step. Then, eventually, I asked Him to teach me how to thrive, not just survive. God was faithful, guiding me from "why" to "survive" to "thrive."

Because I chose to trust Him, He opened doors for me to lead grief groups and work with women who had lost children or struggled with infertility. They saw that I still had hope and joy despite my loss, and I could speak into their lives and love them through their struggles.

That chapter of my journey taught me how to care for people who were hurting. As Scott and I continued moving forward, God faithfully guided us step by step. We didn't know where the journey would take us, but we knew He would help us through it.

One image that God gave me during this time was the picture of God holding my hand as I grasped a thorny stem; my hand bleeding from the pain of losing my boys was all I could see. Over time, He gently pulled my hand back, revealing a beautiful rose at the top of the stem. My pain wasn't for nothing. He could use it to help others if I allowed Him to.

Faithfulness and Next Steps

After a couple of months, I still wanted to be a mother. Scott and I discussed whether we should try to get pregnant again, but after trying some fertility treatments, I realized I couldn't go through it again. My body, mind, and spirit were exhausted. God eventually directed me to seminary, and we moved to South Carolina after I finished, where I became a church's children's pastor and business administrator.

When we made the move, we told God, "Wherever You want us to go, we'll go. Whatever positions You want us to have, we'll take." God kept opening doors for children's ministry positions, which surprised me. I had been working in the singles ministry and had always wanted my own children, not three hundred other people's kids. However, that's the job He gave me, and I ended up loving it. I did go back to God and clarify that I still wanted my *own* children, too.

Working with children and managing the business side of the church became a great blessing. Scott volunteered in the children's ministry, where he discovered he had a gift for teaching kids, even though they had always intimidated him. He became a large-group teacher, a role he's now filled for nearly thirty years.

As we settled into this new phase of life, there was still a longing for kids and, ultimately, grandkids. We began to consider adoption. We hadn't thought about it much before, but we knew we could either spend thousands of dollars on fertility treatments with no guarantee of success or we could invest those resources into adopting children who needed loving homes.

We started researching adoption, even though we had no idea what we were doing. We connected with CPS, filled out the application, and waited. However, the process wasn't as smooth as we hoped. The caseworker told us that if we were looking to adopt a white child under the age of two, we'd be waiting forever. I told her, "I think you missed something on our application. We're open to adopting a sibling group, any race or ethnicity, and older children."

Eventually, we realized that CPS wouldn't be an easy route, so we found Bethany Christian Services, a subcontractor with the state. There, we connected with Burt Fields, a wonderful woman who helped guide us through the process. With her help, we qualified and began looking for children available for adoption nationwide.

We found a sibling group of four in South Carolina, but the state would not allow us to pursue them. So, we began looking outside the state and found a sibling group of four in Tennessee. Shortly after, someone sent us information about a sibling group of five in Tennessee. The paperwork for the group of four in Tennessee indicated that they should not be kept together due to the potential for endangering the children if they remained as a unit.

Scott, Burt, and I made the difficult decision to decline to pursue that group. It was incredibly hard to say no, especially when you deeply desire children, but we knew it wasn't the right choice for us or them.

Next, we considered the sibling group of five—three boys and two girls. This group turned out to be a perfect fit for us. We started the paperwork and moved forward with meeting the children. Overnight, we went from no children to five. We brought home our "basketball team," as we joked.

The first day the children were in our home, it became clear they already knew how to play with each other. They were six, seven, eight, nine, and ten years old at the time. The youngest came up to me after playing outside for a few hours and asked, "What's for dinner?" This cute little boy looked up at me, and I realized I was completely unprepared. I thought, *Do you ask this question every day?*

That's when my master's in organizational management kicked in. We began creating food plans, clothes plans, and laundry systems. Everything needed a system, and we implemented them quickly.

These children had been living in two different foster homes. One of the foster families had done an amazing job helping four of our children heal from their past trauma. The other foster home for our daughter was a therapeutic home that did not have the nurture that she needed. These children filled our home with wonder and excitement, though we understood there would be inevitable challenges.

As we navigated parenting our children, we quickly learned what it means to care for kids who have experienced trauma. These children had endured things no child should ever experience, including abuse and neglect. Scott and I had to get healthy and stable quickly to be the parents they needed.

We also had to adjust our parenting styles. Traditional methods often don't work with children who have been through trauma. Our children viewed the world through trauma lenses. Sometimes, if I moved too fast, they would flinch, thinking they might be hit, even though I would never hurt them. Their past experiences taught them to expect that kind of treatment.

We learned a lot from our kids; they helped us grow as parents. Shortly after the children moved in with us, Scott had to return to work in Houston while we stayed in South Carolina. I essentially became a single parent, which created all kinds of fun scenarios as we learned to become a family. After the adoption was finalized, we joined Scott in Houston.

Parenting came with ups and downs, as we faced challenges such as children making poor decisions, lashing out, and harsh words directed at us. Through it all, we learned to love as Jesus loves—unconditionally, even when things don't go right. My role as a mom became clear: my job is to plant positive seeds and point my children to Jesus. I can't control their behavior or their choices, but I can influence them by loving them and providing guidance.

About seven years after our first adoption, I felt God calling us to adopt again. We had plenty of space in our home, and I believed we were being asked to be obedient in expanding our family. While attending a conference in Georgia, I heard Francis Chan speak about a couple in a third-world country who were caring for orphans despite their limited resources.

As Francis spoke, I thought about our home and how, if we rearranged things, we could house up to fourteen kids. The thought seemed crazy, but the story of the couple deeply inspired me. Francis concluded by saying, "None of us would want to be that couple now, given the heartache and cost, but all of us would want to be them when they stand before Jesus and hear, 'Well done, good and faithful servant.'"

After the conference, I called Scott and told him I thought we were supposed to adopt again. His response was, "Uh, no thanks. Feel free to stay gone as long as you need." I replied, "You need to pray about it."

When I returned home, we discussed it further, and Scott eventually agreed after 6 weeks to bring it up with the kids. To our surprise, they were all excited about the idea. We talked about the sacrifices involved, like sharing toys and rooms, and my daughter, who played select softball, recognized that she might have to give up the sport due to the cost.

I also told the kids, "We might not be able to pay for college, cars, or weddings. These are things we may have to sacrifice. Are you okay with that?" They all said yes. So, Scott and I decided to submit our application. Within six months, we had two more children, ages eleven and thirteen, joining our family.

Suddenly, we had children aged eleven, thirteen, fourteen, fifteen, sixteen, seventeen, and eighteen. Hormones and driver's education became our new reality. Mixing children from different sibling groups, all with trauma backgrounds, brought its own set of challenges.

One of our first adopted children, who was fourteen and the baby of the bunch, was excited that he would be a big brother to our new thirteen-year-old son. Unfortunately for him, our new thirteen-year-old son was an oldest sibling, and he was much more interested in hanging out with my oldest son and asking me for my car keys and money. My fourteen-year-old just wanted to play Legos. So obviously, not everything was a smooth transition; we all needed lots of grace and patience with each other.

There were also difficult moments when the children would say, "You're not my sibling," and we had to work through those feelings. However, we committed to being a family—blood didn't matter. We didn't always like each other, but we loved each other.

As the kids grew older and started to move out, we faced even more challenges. Some fell into drugs and prostitution, and others made harsh decisions. However, these experiences taught me compassion and allowed me to walk alongside my children in their struggles. This reminded me regularly that my only job was to plant a positive seed and leave a bridge to Jesus. We were required to trust God and stretch and grow along the journey.

One of my older daughters returned to her biological mother and became pregnant. At the time, we thought her baby might end up in CPS custody, so I felt God nudging us to get our paperwork ready, just in case. My husband thought I was crazy. I told him to pray about it because God either wants us to be willing to adopt again or be willing to step in with this grandchild—or He has something else for us. My husband prayed and, six months later, agreed that we should turn our paperwork in to be ready and available for whatever God had next. Praise God our grandbaby didn't end up in CPS custody; we did adopt another sibling group though—a nine-year-old and an eleven-year-old giving us a grand total of nine children.

Through this process, I discovered Dr. Karen Purvis' Trust Based Relational Intervention work on helping children with trauma backgrounds. Her research transformed the way I connected with my children and profoundly impacted the work we would later do at Anchor Point.

Adoption wasn't originally our plan, but it became our plan A, and God has used it to grow us as a family and teach us how to love as He loves. We've faced many difficulties, but I wouldn't change a thing.

My children have made their share of bad decisions. Some of our kids have dealt with drugs, crime, and other hardships, but they are still my kids. My job is to plant seeds and point them to Jesus. God is writing a good story in their lives, and I'm praying to live long enough to see it unfold and asking for wisdom every day.

One of my daughters, who struggled with drugs for many years, is now sober. She holds a job and is pursuing the life God has for her, and I love watching her grow. Being her mama is a joy.

Now, we're on to the next phase: grandkids. They call me "Lolli" and Scott "Pops," and they love visiting Lolli-Pop's house. Grandkids are amazing! One of my grandchildren was so cute as she pondered that if each of my kids had nine children, I would have eighty-one grandchildren. I laughed and said, "Well, if that is the case, we might as well shoot for one hundred."

This journey has been hard, but it's been good. It's been centered in God's will, and we've been blessed and changed for the better because of it. We would do it all over again, even with the highs and lows.

"It is doubtful whether God can bless a man greatly until He has hurt him deeply."

—A.W. Tozer

"Your greatest ministry will likely come from your deepest pain."

—Rick Warren

"Although the world is full of suffering, it is also full of the overcoming of it."

—Helen Keller

Make it Personal

1. What are you currently holding on to that you sense God may be asking you to release?

2. How do you view surrender? Does it come easily, or is it a struggle for you?

3. Reflect on a time when you surrendered something to God. What was the outcome, and how did it impact your faith?

4. What step can you take this week to live out the core message of this chapter and inspire others by example?

5. How can embracing this chapter's theme of surrendering and letting go help you make a difference in your community or in someone else's life?

CHAPTER 4

Anchor Point's Genesis

> "Whatever you do, work at it with all your heart, as working for the Lord, not for human masters, since you know that you will receive an inheritance from the Lord as a reward. It is the Lord Christ you are serving."
>
> —Colossians 3:23–24 NIV

Eternity Focused

A significant shift in my career path and perspective on life occurred after losing our biological boys. I began to view everything through the lens of eternity. I wanted everything I did to have eternal significance, which greatly affected my career at Exxon. I no longer found fulfillment there and started seeking what God was doing and how I could join Him. That eventually led me to seminary and beyond.

Somewhere along the way, I had this thought—it may have been a midlife crisis—about what I was uniquely called and gifted to do. I wondered, *"What could I do that would make a difference for both now and eternity? Could I build something that would outlive me and have an impact for years to come?"*

That's when the idea of Anchor Point was planted in my mind. God began to stir this desire in me, but I resisted. I thought, *Oh my gosh, no way, God.* I had already done church plants, had seven children, and was involved in full-time ministry at home and church. Plus, it would cost time and money. I kept telling God, *No, no, no,* but the feeling wouldn't go away. I knew there was something I needed to do—something that would bring hope to families who were overwhelmed, struggling, or facing unplanned pregnancies and families struggling with adopted children.

I fought this for a long time until I finally felt like God was saying, "Do you have time to work on it now?" I had no choice but to answer, "Yes, I'll do what you want me to do." Ultimately, surrender and humility won the day.

I shared the idea with one of my close friends, Melissa, thinking if she didn't like it, I could dismiss it as my own misguided thoughts. However, she was incredibly excited when I told her about creating something that could help families and make a lasting impact. I thought, *Oh no, God, please no,* but she was all in.

We talked to our pastor, who was also excited about the vision. I felt like I was being dragged into it, yet I knew I had this vision and was supposed to follow through. Melissa's husband Jeff, my husband, and the two of us sat down, formed the corporation, filed for tax exemption, and started planting the seeds for Anchor Point.

Initially, we thought we might focus on children aging out of the foster care system, given my experience with adoption. However, that door kept closing, and we eventually shifted toward supporting birth and adoption, trying to figure out how best to proceed.

We started having conversations with people in our community, gathering a group of pastors to share the vision. They were supportive, though none contributed financially at first. However, they did express a willingness to send people our way as we grew.

We decided to host a community-wide meeting, inviting anyone interested in learning more. Almost 250 people attended. Before the meeting, I asked my friend, "What are we going to say, and who's going to talk?" She said, "You talk," and I thought, *Okay, God, I don't even want to do this. What are we doing?*

I got up in front of the crowd and shared our vision: We were starting with a pregnancy center, and one day, we hoped to have education and counseling services, a maternity home, and a home for children aging out of foster care. We also wanted to educate parents and raise the level of parenting in our community, championing the future of children by empowering their parents. I told them, "No one is beyond hope." People got excited, and many started donating.

Breakthroughs and Gifts

We received our IRS tax exemption approval on the same day as the meeting—the shortest approval time possible. This was during a period when many religious non-profits were facing delays or denials. Ours came through with no questions or issues, and I thought, *Okay, God, we're supposed to be doing this.*

With the support of the community, we kept moving forward. We found a beautiful facility in a strip center with fourteen rooms—more than we thought we'd ever need—and secured it at a great price. One church held a diaper drive for us and filled three of those rooms to the ceiling with supplies.

Step by step, God opened doors and brought to us the clients who needed our services and us.

Looking back, Anchor Point likely wouldn't exist today if we hadn't gone through the loss of our boys. That journey of loss allowed God to redeem our pain and prepare us for the next steps. Walking through adoption and those experiences cultivated in me a heart willing to take on big dreams and big challenges.

Anchor Point was born out of that pain, and God used it to heal our hearts and give us the ability to love again. Anchor Point is a place where people can find love and hope, no matter where they are on their journey or their choices. We will love them and point them to Jesus, their ultimate hope.

"The purpose of your life is far greater than your own personal fulfillment, your peace of mind, or even your happiness. It's far greater than your family, your career, or even your wildest dreams and ambitions."

—Rick Warren

"The people who are crazy enough to think they can change the world are the ones who do."

—Steve Jobs

"We are to live for an audience of one: God alone."

—Oswald Chambers

Make it Personal

1. How do you think focusing on eternity changes the way you live your life today?

2. In what ways do your daily choices reflect eternal values?

3. What do you believe is your unique calling or purpose, and how does it relate to eternity?

4. What step can you take this week to live out the core message of this chapter and inspire others by example?

5. How can embracing this chapter's theme of living with eternity focus help you make a difference in your community or in someone else's life?

CHAPTER 5

Building Anchor Point

"And my God will meet all your needs according to the riches of His glory in Christ Jesus."

—Philippians 4:19

Next Best Steps

One of the most significant considerations is staying faithful and willing to take the next best step in our journey. Even though I was initially reluctant, I remained open to listening to God, exploring opportunities, and seeking affirmation about whether doors should open or close. When God places something on your heart, you must be willing to dig in, explore it, and join Him where He continues to open doors.

For Anchor Point, several doors opened for us from a business perspective. When we filed the paperwork for tax exemption with the IRS, it was in 2010 when many religious non-profits faced delays or denials. Yet, our exemption was approved within ninety days without any issues. That in itself was miraculous.

Before officially starting Anchor Point, as we were laying the groundwork, I had the opportunity to work with a doctor on the other side of town to help him start his medical clinic. That experience was invaluable; it taught me about medical billing, managing a medical office, and many other aspects I hadn't known before. As it turned out, those skills became essential for running Anchor Point.

That relationship with the doctor and his family has remained strong, and he continues to be a significant supporter of Anchor Point to this day.

The fact that people would come together to talk about the possibility of something—and that we could share a dream with them, and they would feel called to be a part of it—was pretty amazing. God opened doors, and everything in this process has been a faith journey. My journey before Anchor Point, learning to trust in faith, was only expanded and strengthened as I navigated the years of building Anchor Point.

Despite having nothing at the time, we found a facility that we could afford, and it was perfect for our first location. A church blessed us with supplies to provide to mothers, and other centers across Texas graciously mentored us on what to do and how to do it. They didn't require us to adopt all their methods but taught us what was working for them and mentored us along the way.

These were all things that God put in place. I didn't know how to do any of this—how to start a business or a ministry or how to raise funds. I had some knowledge, but I had never done it on my own. I had a vision of what we were building but didn't know all the steps to get there. All I knew was to take the next best step and hold my plans loosely, letting God open and close doors as He saw fit. Over the years, I've added a prayer: God, if you are going to close a door, please make sure my fingers are out of the frame, so it's a lot less painful.

We had to stretch, grow, and learn how to persevere. We needed to be focused, faithful, and fearless, and that's what we did. Those traits have been hard-wired into me for most of my life, so it was a natural place to apply them. We began building and volunteering when we could and eventually hired our first staff member. When she transitioned out, the question became, "Who will lead the organization?" And that person ended up being me, even though it wasn't my plan. My plan was only to be on the board of directors for Anchor Point, but now, I would be even more hands-on.

At every turn, God provided great resources, and we kept moving forward, sometimes getting things right and celebrating, and sometimes getting them wrong and picking up the pieces.

Perseverance is required to build and maintain something bigger than any one of us.

Challenges and Funding

One of our biggest challenges was funding. Many people were excited about the ministry but hesitant to contribute financially until they knew we would succeed. For the first three years, money was extremely tight. After three years, churches and individuals began to support us after we proved that we were stably producing good results.

In those early years, we often didn't have enough donations to cover staff salaries. I would write personal checks from our personal bank account to cover the costs. I'd deposit the money into the Anchor Point account and call my husband, saying, "I just wrote a $3,000 (or $5,000) check for Anchor Point." Then, he would ask me if there was money in the bank, and I would say, "I don't know. I didn't look." He would always be supportive, even though we had five (later seven) kids. I'd say, "Don't spend any money," and he'd reply, "Okay." We trusted God to provide, and He always did.

Eventually, we reached a point where I no longer had to write those personal checks to make ends meet, and I wasn't working for free anymore. That was a huge relief and a sign that the organization was on more stable ground. God faithfully cared for Anchor Point and our family throughout the journey.

Hearts of Love and Touched Lives

This ministry deals with orphans and children caught between life and death, both of which are close to God's heart. He is at the center of it, and we've been able to trust Him throughout the process. Even though we didn't always know how we would make it, we've seen life after life saved and changed for eternity, making it all worth it.

I remember one woman who cried every time I spoke about Anchor Point. It turned out that she had an abortion forty years earlier and had kept it a secret all that time. Every day, she thought about the child she aborted. She was one of the first women to go through our abortion recovery class, and I watched as years of pain and shame lifted off her. She later became a leader in that class and has helped many women heal.

Another young woman chose life for her child during a crisis pregnancy. Later, financial pressures led her to choose abortion for her second pregnancy. Despite disagreeing with her decision, we loved and continued supporting her. She became pregnant a third time, came back to us, and chose life again. She now has two beautiful children and one child in heaven.

Stories like these remind me that all of this has been worth it. God created a heart in me to serve, and even when I was reluctant, He faithfully guided me. We've continued to expand Anchor Point's services, including opening a maternity home for homeless women, helping them figure out how to provide for themselves and their children while also finding spiritual support.

It's been an incredible journey, one that has required me to be focused, fearless, and faithful. We've built a million-dollar organization, but more importantly, it's an eternal business. The lives we get to touch make all the hard work, challenges, and uncertainties worth it.

You can learn more about Anchor Point and some of the lives impacted for eternity in the appendix of this book.

> "Trust God to weave your thread into the great web, though the pattern shows it not yet."
>
> —Charles Spurgeon

> "Relying on God has to begin all over again every day as if nothing had yet been done."
>
> —C.S. Lewis

> "Faith is taking the first step even when you don't see the whole staircase."
>
> —Martin Luther King Jr.

Make it Personal

1. Think of a recent decision you made. How did you determine the "next best step"?

2. What steps could you take to seek God's guidance more intentionally in your decision-making?

3. How do you handle uncertainty in decision-making, and how might you improve this process?

4. What step can you take this week to live out the core message of this chapter and inspire others by example?

5. How can embracing this chapter's theme of taking the next best step help you make a difference in your community or in someone else's life?

CHAPTER 6

Personal Growth Through Your Journey

"I have been crucified with Christ, and I no longer live, but Christ lives in me. The life I now live in the body, I live by faith in the Son of God, who loved me and gave Himself for me."

—Galatians 2:20

Falling in Love with Jesus

I have experienced many things since that week in VBS so long ago, but one area of growth that continues to develop for me is understanding what it means to fall in love with Jesus and to walk out my relationship with Him. Growth comes the more I realize and hold on to the truth that it is not about me and my wants. Instead, we have the opportunity to be part of His story and what He is doing in the world.

I love what Henry Blackaby says about looking for where God is at work and joining Him there. It's not about me; it's about God, bringing Him glory, and pointing others to Him.

We have the unique privilege of doing that. To do it well, my identity in Christ must be solid because, by nature, I am a very selfish person who likes things my way.

However, God asks me to lay down my desires, pick up His way, and follow Him. That often means stepping into hard things, suffering, and trusting Him when the way isn't clear. It means choosing the difficult path when I'd much rather take the easy one.

For example, people often ask why we don't travel more, and I laugh and say, "Oh, I've traveled plenty—through my children. That's where we've invested our resources." It's funny because it's different from what many expect.

Some friends can't wait to retire, but I've come to understand that retirement, as we think of it, isn't biblical. We may not continue our careers forever, but we are still on God's mission field. It's not about settling down with a great house, porch, and coffee, letting life pass by. It's about how many people we can impact for God, sharing His love and showing them the way.

An Audience of One

Over time, I've come to understand that I perform for an audience of One. The decisions I make—whether in ministry, business or with my family—are ultimately for God, not for others. When people don't like my decisions, it doesn't change my values or what I'm called to do. As long as I am confident that I've sought His wisdom and guidance, I can trust He will handle everything accordingly.

Having my identity grounded in Christ makes a difference in everything I do. Has it evolved over time? Absolutely. I've learned and grown, becoming more attuned to what God wants for me. I've realized that God is more interested in our journey than in the tasks we complete. Am I growing to look more like Him as I age? Do I display love, joy, peace, patience, kindness, goodness, faithfulness, gentleness, and self-control? Do I have compassion for others, even when they're unkind?

Humility and Surrender

The recurring themes in my life have been humility and surrender. God wants humility and surrender from me, and He wants them from all of us. When I approach life humbly, I remain open to learning, growing, and compassionately understanding others. A surrendered life means holding things loosely, stepping into hard places, and trusting God with my life, my plans, and what He has for me to accomplish.

Over the past three years, God has emphasized the importance of how I care for my body—the temple of the Holy Spirit. The Bible teaches that our bodies are temples, and we must take care of them physically, mentally, emotionally, and spiritually. I've always been driven and willing to take on challenges, but sometimes, that has led to depletion. Whether it was being overweight, stressed, or otherwise out of control, God has made it clear that I must take better care of myself to care for others.

This realization came during a stressful time post-COVID when I was dealing with an employee lawsuit, working long hours, raising nine children, with some living on the streets and others facing different challenges. I had grandbabies born out of wedlock, and life was chaotic. One day, I shut a truck door on my leg, creating a wound that refused to heal. I developed a staph infection, and despite visiting a wound doctor, nothing worked.

It wasn't until I started working with a nutritionist that the wound healed naturally in about fifty-four days. From that point forward, this led to two and a half years of working on my health—changing my diet, exercising, managing stress, and trusting God more fully. I realized that if my life is stressful, I need to find peace by trusting God in all situations.

Mentally, I focus on centering my life on Christ, filling my mind with positive thoughts, and speaking life-giving words. God has challenged me in all areas—physically, mentally, emotionally, and spiritually—to treat my body as a temple for the Holy Spirit. I now understand that if I don't take care of myself, I can't be the person I need to be in my personal life, business, ministry, or family.

One of my favorite things to say, especially to my staff or kids when facing challenges, is, "No worries, God's got this." It's a reminder that He's in control and will show us the way through. I often don't know how we'll handle something, but I know that God does. Another phrase I often use is, "What's the next best step?" We may not know the whole plan, but we can take the next best step and trust God to lead us.

These phrases—"No worries, God's got it" and "What's the next best step?"—have become my guiding principles. By taking care of myself, living in humility, and surrendering my plans, I give God fertile ground to work in my life, using me in ways I could never have imagined.

> "The most important thing in your life is not what you do; it's who you become. That's what you will take into eternity."
> —Dallas Willard

> "Humility is nothing but the disappearance of self in the vision that God is all."
> —Andrew Murray

> "What lies behind us and what lies before us are tiny matters compared to what lies within us."
> —Ralph Waldo Emerson

Make it Personal

1. In what ways have you grown personally through difficult experiences?

2. Reflect on an area of your life where you are seeking to grow. What steps are you taking to reach that goal?

3. How do you approach situations that challenge your comfort zone?

4. What step can you take this week to live out the core message of this chapter and inspire others by example?

5. How can embracing this chapter's theme of personal growth help you make a difference in your community or in someone else's life?

CHAPTER 7

Looking Ahead

"Brothers and sisters, I do not consider myself yet to have taken hold of it. But one thing I do: Forgetting what is behind and straining toward what is ahead, I press on toward the goal to win the prize for which God has called me heavenward in Christ Jesus."

—Philippians 3:13–14

One of the most interesting aspects of life is the ongoing opportunity to reinvent ourselves and expand into who we are meant to be, according to God's calling. It's always a meaningful endeavor to ask, "God, what else do you have for me? How can I serve you and become the legacy maker you want me to be?" These are powerful questions that allow God to shape us into who He needs us to be if we are brave and willing. This means our lives will continue to grow and change.

I have always found it difficult to settle for the status quo. This spurs that question: "God, what else do you have for me?" As I reflect on how He continues to shape me, I see an ever-growing opportunity to broaden awareness of Anchor Point and extend its impact.

Beyond that, I am also energized by the chance to come alongside others, wherever they may be, guiding them through the process of building their legacies. I am encouraged by the possibilities to share what I have learned and to help others discover how they can make a meaningful difference in their businesses, families, and personal lives.

I believe that when we wholeheartedly follow God and pursue lives of significance, we become Kingdom-impact players, leaving lasting imprints that glorify Him.

Through Anchor Point, and in the many connections I make along the way, I remain watchful for opportunities to guide and inspire others, offering fresh ways to extend a ripple effect of hope and transformation. At Anchor Point, every time a mother chooses life, those ripples stretch into future generations, creating legacies that touch countless lives.

This work is not just about what we achieve today; it is about laying a foundation for those who will follow. I believe that as we continue to nurture legacy builders, we bring joy to the heart of our Heavenly Father. It is a privilege to be part of this ongoing story, faithfully taking the next best step and marveling at what God unfolds along the way. This will also create wonderful opportunities for those who come after us. I believe that when we do this right, it makes our Heavenly Father smile.

> "You don't have to know a lot of things for your life to make a lasting difference in the world. But you do have to know the few great things that matter, perhaps just one, and be willing to live for them and die for them."
> —John Piper

> "Twenty years from now you will be more disappointed by the things you didn't do than by the ones you did

do. So throw off the bowlines. Sail away from the safe harbor. Catch the trade winds in your sails. Explore. Dream. Discover."

—Mark Twain

"The people who are crazy enough to think they can change the world are the ones who do."

—Steve Jobs

Make it Personal

1. What dreams or goals are you pursuing that you believe align with God's purpose for you?

2. How do you balance planning for the future while remaining present in your current season?

3. What legacy do you hope to leave, and how are you taking steps toward that vision?

4. What step can you take this week to live out the core message of this chapter and inspire others by example?

5. How can embracing this chapter's theme of looking ahead help you make a difference in your community or in someone else's life?

PART 2
Lessons Learned

As I continue to consider what it means to leave a legacy, I have continued to circle back to three characteristics that God has encouraged me to lean into: remaining focused, faithful, and fearless.

When I think about remaining focused, I think about keeping my eyes on the goal and being able to see the end clearly. Being faithful means being committed, dependable, and unwavering—always present, no matter the circumstances. Finally, being fearless doesn't mean being reckless or taking unnecessary risks. Instead, it means being willing to take on challenges, confront hard situations, and do what needs to be done. My fear is not eliminated, but I fear less what the world thinks of me and focus more on what God thinks of me.

In the chapters that follow, I'd like to share how these characteristics provide a foundation for many legacy making opportunities in every area of life with the hope that you will be encouraged to lean into these in your own journey.

SECTION 1
Focused

CHAPTER 8

Know the End Goal

"You will keep in perfect peace those whose minds are steadfast, because they trust in you."

—Isaiah 26:3

When we talk about being focused, one of the most important aspects is **knowing our goals**. What are we trying to accomplish? To stay focused, we need clear, actionable goals. Having an overarching goal is essential, but we also need to break it down into steps that will allow us to achieve it. Then, we must remain flexible as we walk forward in faith, keeping our eyes focused on God.

Anchor Point's Vision and Process

Early at Anchor Point, we sketched a picture of what we envisioned for the organization. This included a pregnancy help center, a maternity home for pregnant and homeless girls, a home for children aging out of foster care, and a program to educate parents to help them succeed. This vision was created when we were filing for tax exemption with the IRS, and it became the foundation for what we talked about as our goal and dream.

With this big, overarching goal in mind, we took a step back to consider what we could realistically accomplish first. Initially, we thought we would start by working with children aging out of foster care, but God kept closing those doors. So, we shifted our focus to other areas of the vision where doors were opening. God led us to work with young women struggling with the decision to choose life for the child they carried.

We asked ourselves: How could we come alongside them? How could we let them see their babies, hear their heartbeats, and show them their options while providing the assistance they needed? We broke this goal down into small, manageable steps. Along the way, we made mistakes and had successes, but the key was learning quickly and adjusting as we grew.

As we progressed, we discovered new opportunities and additional services we could offer. By enlisting volunteers to help with tasks, we freed up time and resources to accomplish even bigger parts of our dream. We began to pull more people into the vision. I focused on delegating tasks that others could do, allowing me to focus on the responsibilities only I, as the CEO, could handle.

This is how we used the concept of goal-setting—by writing down our goals, having a clear vision, and continually striving to move forward.

Our Family's Goals and the Importance of Relationship

When we consider our family, one of our primary goals has been to maintain heartfelt connections and open relationships with our children. While I knew that academic success was important and wanted my children to do well in school, the relational aspect was even more crucial for me. If my children knew how to give and receive care, function well in groups and by themselves, and use their words to express their needs, they could succeed in almost any endeavor they pursued.

These relational aspects were very important to me because the world competes for the hearts of our children. We prioritized staying connected with our children, regardless of their decisions—whether good or poor—as they navigated life. We wanted them to know that our home was a safe place where they could always come to us. This doesn't mean they always received the answers they wanted, but they knew they could always come to us and find truth, unconditional love, and support in figuring out their best next steps.

Our goals as parents have always been clear: to plant positive seeds in our children at every opportunity and to build a bridge pointing them to Jesus. We believe that Jesus is the answer to the significant issues they face in life and to all the challenges they encounter. If they embrace this truth, everything else will fall into place.

Personal Goals

Regarding my personal life goals, it has been important for me to understand how God has given me the opportunity—through the presence of the Holy Spirit within me—to care for the body He has entrusted to me in many ways: mentally, emotionally, physically, and spiritually. I believe the spiritual aspect is the most important, as everything else flows from it.

My relationship with Jesus Christ has set the course for my life. As I continue to pursue Him, He reveals my next steps. Over time, I have grown more comfortable with humility and surrender, learning to follow where He leads and to trust His direction. This has not always been easy, but I have improved as I have walked this path. The important part is to focus, regardless of even big setbacks, on following once more.

Spiritually, my foundation is that Jesus is the center of my life. I want everything I do to be rooted in God's Word. I seek to know Him with my whole heart and ask myself: *Am I producing fruit? Does my life demonstrate love, joy, peace, patience, kindness, goodness, faithfulness, gentleness, and self-control? Am I pointing others to Him? Am I challenging them to grow deeper in their relationship with Jesus, encouraging and empowering them along the way?*

When my spiritual life is in alignment, I find that the mental component naturally follows. Scripture speaks clearly about taking thoughts captive and choosing words carefully. Do I speak life or death—whether to myself, others, or my children? Emotionally, when I trust Him, my love tank remains full, allowing me to extend love even when others are not kind.

Finally, there's the physical aspect. How do I keep my body healthy so I can be who God needs me to be? I want to remain active and present for many years, making a lasting impact. I shared earlier about my leg injury, which was a pivotal moment in my life when I could have easily faced a much worse outcome. Through that experience, God led me on a journey of learning to care for my body and recognizing how wonderfully it is designed. By becoming more attuned to my body and making an effort to care for it, I can make a bigger impact and remain here longer to influence and lead others to Him.

Challenges and Obstacles

One of the challenges we face, whether personally or in business, is staying true to the vision despite obstacles. In business, as I mentioned earlier, we initially planned to start in one direction, but God closed those doors and led us down a different path. We had to remain faithful to the overarching vision while adjusting to the challenges and changes along the way.

I believe you should prayerfully have a big, dream-driven goal, put it out there, and then start walking toward it, taking the next best step you know. I've learned not to hold my thoughts and dreams too tightly but to leave them to God. I trust the Creator, knowing He may have something slightly or totally different in mind. He's placed this dream in my heart, so I can trust that it will work out somehow. However, the journey might look different than I expected, and He is very interested in how I learn to be humble and surrender to Him.

When I set out on the next best step, my goal is to say, "Okay, God, here's the next best step I know, and this is what I'm going to do." So, I start moving in that direction, holding loosely to my plans, trusting that God will lead and direct me as needed. If I start my day that way, with my big goals in mind, I can view anything that comes into my day not as an interruption meant to derail me but as an opportunity where God is at work—and I need to be aware and ready to join Him.

For example, I may be focused on an important task, and a staff member comes in having a difficult day and is overwhelmed. My fleshly tendency can sometimes be to stay focused on the wrong thing. It is absolutely right to stop and love on them. I'm still pursuing my big goal, but I also need to ensure my people are okay. If that takes an hour or two, so be it. Whether it's an unexpected visit from the IRS or a lawsuit, I remind myself that God knew I'd face this today. Since He knew, I just need to breathe and trust that He has everything under control.

In my family, my kids have made a lot of challenging decisions, as I've shared earlier. It wasn't part of my plan to have a child involved in prostitution. That took me by surprise, but some of her wayward choices led her there. I had to remember that my job as her mother was to maintain that heart connection. If I lost that connection, we might lose her to the world entirely—and possibly to death. Thankfully, she's no longer involved in that life and is figuring her way.

There were many times when she would call and try to shock me with what she said. I would respond, "You know I love you. I don't agree with your choices, but I'm here for you. Call me when you are ready to do the hard work, and I'll help you." We continued to have conversations like that.

I remember one time when I felt convicted about the need to speak the truth to her. I had avoided doing it, concerned that I'd lose our connection and ultimately lose her. But God challenged me to be fearless, to be the mom she needed me to be, and to stand in the gap for her. The next time she called, I asked, "Do you know I love you?"

This was during her time on the streets. She said, "Yes." I asked again, "Do you know that I love you no matter what you're doing or where you're living?" She said, "Yes." I pressed further, "Are you sure?" She confirmed, "Yes."

Then, I told her, "I haven't been the mom you need me to be, and I owe you an apology." She was confused and asked, "What?" I explained, "Sometimes, I don't say things you need to hear because I'm afraid I'll lose you. But God has been convicting me because I need to be the mom who tells you the hard truths."

I went on, "Sometimes, there will be things you don't agree with or want to hear, but I need to be a place where you can count on hearing the truth. Where else in your life do you have people who love you and will tell you the truth?"

She responded, "I don't have anyone."

I said, "I know. And I want to be that person. Your dad and I will be those people for you. That's who we are." From that point on, I would tell her anything. I'd say the hard things she didn't want to hear. She wasn't always happy about it, but she knew we were there for her, that we loved her, and that when she hit bottom, we'd be the ones she could call.

That's not what I'd consider the ideal parent-child relationship, but it's about sticking with it through the challenges. We had another child who spent years on the streets, caught in drug addiction and poor choices. The police would call us, and we had hard choices to make not to enable her behavior.

Each time she was detoxed in the hospital, she would call us. We'd bring her whatever she needed, and then, before she was discharged, we'd ask if she was ready to go to rehab. Time and again, she said no. We'd respond, "When you're ready, let us know." That cycle went on for years. It was incredibly hard.

That child is now clean and sober and has held down a job for several years. It's because we never forgot the end goal. We continued to plant positive seeds and left a bridge to Jesus so that she could find her way in the world. She is a joy to be with today.

We could go on with story after story about my children. It's during the hard times that we truly learn and grow. The good times are easier—we can celebrate those, and planting positive seeds and pointing them to Jesus is sweet in those moments. But it's in the hard times when life really plays out, and you learn who you can count on and who will be there for you.

In my personal life, I've learned the most by staying true to following Jesus. One of the key lessons is that I don't get to dictate what will become of my life. My life exists to glorify Him and to bring others to Him. While I might have a dream of what I think is ideal, that may not be what's truly best for me. I can trust that God has the absolute best for me.

As I've walked through life, my end goal is to hear Him say, when I get to heaven, that I've done a good job and been a good and faithful servant. Not perfect, but good and faithful with the things He's given me: the time, the talents, and the opportunities.

The concepts of humility and surrender are central to this. I'm learning to ask God, "What do You want me to do today? What's the most important thing?" and "Are there things in my life that are distracting me?" Asking these kinds of questions sets me up for success when I face challenges.

I remember receiving the lawsuit at Anchor Point and thinking, *What am I supposed to do with this? How do I figure my way through?* Time and again, in family, business, and personal matters, I've found myself crying out to God, saying, "I don't know how to get through this. I don't just want to survive—I want to thrive. Show me how."

Turning to Him, knowing He is always here, never surprised, and always for me, is what has allowed me to walk through challenges, conquer new ones, and continue to expand and do the things I'm called to do.

"If you aim at nothing, you'll hit it every time."

—Zig Ziglar

"Success demands singleness of purpose."

—Vince Lombardi

"Success is not final, failure is not fatal: It is the courage to continue that counts."

—Winston Churchill

Make it Personal

1. What do you believe is your "end goal" in life, and how does it shape your choices?

2. How do you keep your focus on the big picture during daily challenges and distractions?

3. Are there any areas where you feel misaligned with your end goal? How might you realign them?

4. What step can you take this week to live out the core message of this chapter and inspire others by example?

5. How can embracing this chapter's theme of knowing the end goal help you make a difference in your community or in someone else's life?

CHAPTER 9

Eliminate Distractions

> "Let your eyes look straight ahead; fix your gaze directly before you. Give careful thought to the paths for your feet and be steadfast in all your ways. Do not turn to the right or the left; keep your foot from evil."
>
> —Proverbs 4:25–27

Another concept I've relied on to stay focused over the years—in business, family, and personal life—has been eliminating distractions and managing my time effectively by prioritizing tasks that help maintain focus.

We need to understand that everything is out to distract us, even our minds. If we have big goals, big dreams, and big things we want to accomplish, we must become skilled at eliminating distractions.

The Bible says that Satan prowls around, looking to seek, kill, and destroy. He seeks ways to infiltrate our lives, families, and businesses to distract and destroy. His greatest success wouldn't be in eliminating us but in making us ineffective during our time on earth. We must remain aware of this and be vigilant in guarding against it.

Time Management in Business

One common strategy is effective time management. As mentioned in the previous chapter, having goals and knowing the endgame is essential in business, specifically at Anchor Point, as well as in other ministry and business situations over the years. However, we also need to guard against mission creep.

Throughout our journey, numerous opportunities arose—many of them good, some even great—but they were slightly off-focus from our core objectives. For instance, at one point, Anchor Point brought a school under its umbrella, which initially aligned well with our mission of helping families and children dealing with trauma. It seemed like a great opportunity to elevate families to the next level. However, over time, the school came to require disproportionally more time, finances, and energy compared to our core mission and needed more dedicated attention. This made moving forward with our primary objectives increasingly difficult. The board and I had to make the hard decision to step back and consider launching the school as its own 501(c)(3) entity, allowing it to stand on its own. One of our partner churches was very interested in helping with this process. Together, we successfully launched the school as an independent organization, and it is thriving today. We still contribute by helping train and develop its leaders, but releasing it allowed the school to get the focused attention it needed and Anchor Point to refocus on our primary mission.

The outcome was remarkable, as God used this process to launch a second ministry. These two ministries are now sister organizations that support each other, enabling them both to grow and thrive. This experience taught us the importance of recognizing when a good thing is better off in the hands of others to take ownership and elevate it to the next level and refocus our time.

As we initially planned when we started Anchor Point, we wanted a maternity home at some point. We knew that homeless pregnant girls were at great risk and needed support. We were at the start of COVID-19, and I was extremely overworked and tired. I knew that if we were ever going to accomplish expanding to include a maternity home, God would have to send me a big sign. Well, that sign came in the form of a lady calling one day and saying God told me to build a maternity home, and I just need to find a place to partner with that can help us get it done. I was shocked! This sweet lady did all the legwork and fundraising work to make Anchor Point's dream of Hope House a reality. I could have never done it without her. I realize that I must be aware of the people that God is bringing into my life to help impact even more people. There is something powerful when we can work together in unity and prayer to see God get all the glory and lives changed.

An essential aspect of effective time management is empowering individuals within the organization to take ownership of meaningful roles, regardless of size. Every task contributes to our overall mission, but as a leader, my focus must be on vision, growth, and connecting key individuals to our purpose. By establishing clear systems of reporting and responsibility, I can step back from handling every detail—like being in the client room or managing day-to-day operations—and instead dedicate time to seeking God's direction, anticipating future opportunities, and preparing for challenges ahead. When everyone grows in their ownership, the entire organization flourishes.

Finding committed volunteers and staff members who can manage these day-to-day responsibilities is vital so the key leader can focus on the broader vision.

Schedules, Time Management, and Family Life

On the family side, effective time management is just as important. In a household of nine children and two adults (not even counting the dogs), it's essential to create structure. Our children need both high structure and high nurture. They need systems and processes to help them accomplish tasks, along with a loving, fun environment in which to do so. This principle applies no matter how many children you have.

We found that a schedule was crucial. In our home, we broke the day down into thirty-minute or hour-long increments, providing the structure our kids needed to manage their time effectively. Children don't innately understand how to manage time; it's a skill we must teach them so they can become more effective.

Each morning, the kids would work with me to set their schedule. During the school year, school occupied most of their day, but when they came home, we had a schedule for the evening, as well as for weekends and summer.

Every thirty minutes to an hour was accounted for. The kids knew what needed to be accomplished and helped create the schedule themselves. It included tasks I needed done: chores, helping with dinner, cleaning the kitchen, or doing homework. It also included things they wanted or needed to do, like computer time, watching a TV show, or playing outside.

The schedule covered everything, from bedtime routines to morning wakeups. There were specific days for washing clothes and completing chores. The structure wasn't meant to be overly rigid; it was meant to create freedom.

One funny incident happened when my kids stayed with their grandparents. They woke up and asked, "What's the schedule?" My parents, who hadn't lived that way, were confused. My kids loved the structure of a schedule. They put their schedules on the counter, set a timer or bell, and began their day. They knew exactly what they were doing for each hour. The timer would go off, and they'd move to the next task, which included fun activities like swimming.

They generally got what they wanted, and I got what I needed, making it a great system. This structure allowed them to manage their time independently and reduced their need to constantly ask me what was next. It also freed up my time, especially since I often worked from a home office. Keeping them focused on their tasks was essential.

As I shared with you, my children came from traumatic early years before they came into our family. One of the most important things we as parents can do is be a safe space where our kids can feel comfortable enough to let down their protective walls and work through their trauma histories. Learning there are safe people and that vulnerability can be good is a hard thing for a child, especially when those closest to you who are supposed to love and protect you are often part of the trauma you suffered.

The way we accomplish this environment is by pushing away all the distractions and connecting with this child deeply. Connection mainly happens when I laugh and play with my children. When my children can see that I find them precious and delight in being with them, it is then that they begin to feel safe and may venture into some of those hard stories in their lives. It is in sharing those hard times and having a mom who looks at you and says that you are still special, still loved, and we are going to figure our way through together is the most powerful way to healing.

Our kids must always know that we are for them and will not let anything distract us from meaningfully connecting and walking alongside them. It is in this environment that they will thrive.

Personal Time Management and Planning

From a life and personal perspective, I make a point of asking God what He wants me to be doing and to show me what I need to do. I plan my days, and when I do, I place my schedule before Him and say, "I've planned my day; now You direct my path as I go through it." I approach each day with what I believe are the next best steps.

This practice has been immensely helpful for me as a mother of nine, as a CEO, and in managing my personal life. Knowing my priorities, structuring them well, and staying focused are essential. That does not mean I cannot have downtime or moments for self-care—I absolutely need that, and building those into the schedule is crucial. Interestingly, this approach also better prepares me for God-is-moving interruptions. Since I have already surrendered "my plan" to Him, I am not left wondering about the impact of changes; I trust Him to guide my focus as He shifts it.

At the same time, I stay mindful of the specific objectives I am working toward and the reasons behind them, which give me the energy and strength to accomplish them. Giving my schedule to God and identifying which tasks are most important are my two key strategies for eliminating distractions.

The Importance of Prioritizing Tasks

Another key to eliminating distractions is prioritizing tasks. I plan my days as best I can, then give the rest to God, trusting Him to direct my steps. Proverbs 3:5–6 promises that He will guide us if we trust Him, and that has been the foundation of how I balance my life.

It's also vital to prioritize self-care within this structure. I need to ensure I'm building in time for myself, whether it's downtime or moments to recharge. I might not get a lot of it every day, but I make sure to get some. When my children were younger, making sure I stayed healthy so I could be fully present for them was an especially important priority.

When teaching our kids to prioritize tasks, we emphasized structure and set clear goals for the day. We encouraged them to accomplish those goals, but a key lesson for them was learning to do the hard things first and get them out of the way. For children from trauma backgrounds, the concept of delayed gratification can be particularly difficult, as they may not believe that something good will happen in the future as it often has not in the past. Our daily schedule taught them, "You have your writing assignment, you have your chores, and then, at three o'clock, we go to the swimming pool."

By structuring the day this way, we helped them understand that the reward was coming, so there was no need to become frustrated early in the day. The key question was always, "Are you getting your tasks done so that you can earn the pool time?" This approach helped them grasp the idea that completing hard tasks leads to the fun or desired outcomes.

We set the schedule in a way that reduced conflicts. Instead of constant reminders, I would simply ask, "Did you do what's on the schedule?" If they hadn't, they'd rush to complete their tasks. Similarly, if a task needed to be done before dinner, they knew that they needed to complete it to join the meal. Rather than nagging, I'd say, "Join us for dinner when you're done." Though they might grumble, they'd get the task done and return, and I'd praise them: "I'm so proud of you for staying focused, prioritizing what matters, and getting things done."

These are skills that will benefit them as adults. As I watch them with their children, I see them teaching the same lessons. One of the most precious things I hear from my children is, "Mom, I don't know how you did it, but what you taught us was so valuable." Speaking of delayed gratification… seeing and hearing that is a blessing.

Lastly, in business, the principles of prioritizing tasks and maintaining focus are just as important. We set goals and objectives, but we also ensure accountability. For example, if we're planning a gala and our goal is to have 50 tables of guests, with 60 or 70 percent being new to the ministry, we track progress toward that goal.

Measuring these objectives keeps everyone on track. Communication within the organization is essential, ensuring that everyone understands the goals and stays focused. This helps prevent distractions and ensures that we don't allow other tasks to take priority over our primary objectives.

Once, I had a staff member who was very proud of some of the things she had accomplished. They were all good things, but I sat with her and said, "I need to talk through this with you. These are great. And there is a time and place for this. But do these help us accomplish our current objectives?"

She responded, "Well, no."

I continued, "Exactly. Some of the things you are prioritizing are not helping us reach our overall goal. While they're great things, we need to keep our eyes on our priorities to help us achieve our objective."

We worked together to ensure she understood our priorities and how we went about them. Then, we aligned her time and focus with those priorities so she could succeed within the organization and help the team thrive while accomplishing our goals.

> "Put first things first and we get second things thrown in: put second things first and we lose both first and second things."
>
> —C.S. Lewis

"Focus is about saying no."

—Steve Jobs

"It is not a daily increase, but a daily decrease. Hack away at the inessentials."

—Bruce Lee

Make it Personal

1. What are the main distractions in your life, and how do they affect your goals?

2. How do you stay focused on what truly matters, and what strategies help you avoid distractions?

3. Reflect on a time when you successfully removed a distraction. What difference did it make?

4. What step can you take this week to live out the core message of this chapter and inspire others by example?

5. How can embracing this chapter's theme of eliminating distractions help you make a difference in your community or in someone else's life?

CHAPTER 10

Next Best Step

> "If any of you lacks wisdom, you should ask God, who gives generously to all without finding fault, and it will be given to you."
>
> —James 1:5

Regarding my life, one of the key phrases you'll always hear me say is, "What's the next best step?" This applies to any situation. Whether I'm trying to maintain momentum in my personal life, family, or business or overcome distractions and setbacks, this idea of the next best step has played a crucial role in determining successful outcomes.

Sustaining Momentum in Business

Let's discuss some techniques for sustaining momentum. In business, the best strategy we've employed is adapting our objectives as we grow. God has allowed us to expand the business in various ways, adding different divisions, creating separate companies, and doing interesting things that have helped us grow into a million-dollar ministry, impacting thousands of lives each year.

A key factor in sustaining momentum is regularly assessing our staffing. Are we staffed for success and continued growth? If so, that's great. But we also consider where we foresee growth. If we had additional staff, could we expand our impact? Regularly reviewing this helps us plan for the future.

Additionally, we constantly evaluate what our staff is doing. Are we prioritizing the most important tasks? Is Debbie, as CEO, focusing on the things only she can do? If not, how can we offload tasks to other staff or volunteers so that I can focus on what best serves the organization? These evaluations have been essential in maintaining momentum and fostering growth.

Finally, we are always open to trying new things, even if there's a chance we might fail. If we believe God is leading us, it's not failure; it's part of the learning process. Being faithful to what He calls us to do has been a powerful way to grow, learn, and adjust.

Moving Forward as a Family

Taking calculated steps forward has been a great way for us to continue gaining momentum, expanding our impact, and reaching more people. In our family, one of the things we constantly evaluate is how we can help our children succeed.

We believe that our children need Jesus, and as parents, our responsibility is to plant positive seeds and guide them toward Him, providing a bridge to a relationship with Jesus. This relationship is the best thing for their momentum in life and helps them overcome distractions.

Another important aspect is teaching our children that their story does not define them. Their trauma history is part of their story, but it doesn't have to keep them stuck. We can use it to help them become better, stronger people. As my children have grown, I've learned that one of the best things I can do as a mom is to walk with them through their struggles.

Creating a safe environment where they feel secure has been essential. While I know that my home and life are safe, my children may not always feel that way due to their history. So, my role is to connect with them, pursuing their hearts by showing unconditional love—even when they're upset or saying hurtful things. Often, their words, though harsh, are really a cry for help: "Mom, I need you now more than ever, but I don't know how to tell you." My response has been, "I'm here, and we're going to figure this out together."

This approach, providing a safe place with plenty of structure and nurturing love, has been crucial in helping them through their journey. My children face the same challenges other children do—figuring out high school, learning to drive, deciding what to do with their lives, and making choices. I want to be a mom who says yes as often as possible because yeses build trust and confidence. When I keep in mind on the goal to connect and not on myself, I avoid saying no just because I am tired or frustrated. Instead, I can focus on looking for creative ways to say yes, which also teaches them how to express their needs effectively. If it sounds like I nailed that every time, I have not. But what is our end goal, what are we aiming at, and what are we focusing on? That is critical. Then, we can ensure our focus is on the next best steps.

The Importance of Prayer

When it comes to maintaining momentum in my personal life, it always comes down to my relationship with Jesus and what He is calling me to do. There have been many times when I wasn't sure of the next step, but I've always been willing to ask God for wisdom. He promises to guide us if we are open and willing to be obedient.

For example, when I entered seminary, I prayed that God would open or close doors. I hoped He would close them, as I didn't want to go, but He continued to open them. I also prayed for my husband's job, asking that God provide a position that met specific needs. God answered those prayers, and as He continued to open doors, I realized that my role in sustaining momentum is to surrender and be humble enough to follow His calling.

Whenever we've made big life decisions—whether deciding where to live after seminary or adopting again—we've always put our plans before God. We trusted Him to open or close doors, and He has guided us each step of the way. This has been the key to sustaining momentum in my life. I don't believe I would have adopted a second or third time or started Anchor Point if I hadn't laid those decisions before Him and trusted Him to reveal the next best step.

Over the years, I've learned that God is writing a good story with my life. No matter how easy or difficult it may be, His plan is perfect for me. I want to walk with Him and do what He has called me to do.

Overcoming Distractions and Setbacks

Another key to accomplishing the next best steps is overcoming distractions and setbacks. I have found that He makes a way when I continuously place my plans and challenges before God. Whether it's navigating disagreements with my husband, deciding on a job, or determining whether to pursue having more children, God's guidance has always been my source of strength and direction.

None of these setbacks, distractions, or unexpected events are a surprise to God. So, when a staff member tells me they have another career opportunity to pursue, even though it was a surprise to me, it's not a surprise to Him.

It's no surprise to God when a lawsuit comes into my life through my work. It's no surprise to God when CPS calls because one of my children said something at school that a teacher reported. It's no surprise to God when I lose children. It's no surprise to God when my heart breaks because my child is making terrible choices and living a destructive life, and I fear for them.

None of these things are out of His control.

I have to trust that God is still writing a good story. I have to trust that what God is doing is the absolute best, even when it's hard to see. I think about Paul in the Bible. I don't know if he ever sat in jail thinking, *this is the best story ever.* He suffered through many difficult situations, but the way Paul walked through those challenges made all the difference and influenced people for God.

I want my life to be one that isn't held down by setbacks but one that trusts God is writing a beautiful story. He loves me, cares for me, and will show me the way through.

The same goes for my family. My children have faced many challenges, whether from their past, dealing with biological parents reentering their lives, or facing unresolved trauma. If they don't know the way forward, the question becomes, "What is the next best step?" We seek what feels right and what we believe God is leading us to do. This is how we've navigated their trauma, histories, and just the normal challenges of growing up.

As they've become adults and had their own children, we've continued to walk alongside them, even when they have relationships that may not be the best for them. We always ask, "What's the next best step?"

The same principle applies to business. When distractions or setbacks arise, the key is not to let them take us out. That's where the idea that this is God's ministry or business comes into play—He is in control, and nothing surprises Him. While we may be completely caught off guard, He is not, and we can pause and say, "Okay, God, I don't know what to do." He will guide us. Maybe not immediately, but He will guide us through it.

Another proactive approach to dealing with distractions or setbacks is to anticipate what's coming. For example, we can assess how upcoming legislation, financial changes, or economic trends might affect our organization. Is it an election year? Elections can sometimes create chaos in various areas of the organization.

We plan for this, for example, by creating both an optimistic budget—a dream budget—and a more conservative one based on actual income. Sometimes we meet the full budget, and sometimes we don't. But that's okay because we often accomplish much more than we would have if we'd only dreamed small.

Ultimately, these are the best strategies for figuring out the next best steps, maintaining momentum, and overcoming setbacks and distractions.

> "Our greatest fear should not be of failure but of succeeding at things in life that don't really matter."
>
> —Francis Chan

> "The will of God will not take us where the grace of God cannot sustain us."
>
> —Billy Graham

> "The journey of a thousand miles begins with one step."
>
> —Lao Tzu

Make it Personal

1. How do you approach taking the next step when the future feels uncertain?

2. Describe a time when taking a small, faithful step led to something meaningful. What did you learn?

3. How can you cultivate a habit of trust, even when you can only see one step ahead?

4. What step can you take this week to live out the core message of this chapter and inspire others by example?

5. How can embracing this chapter's theme of embracing the next best step help you make a difference in your community or in someone else's life?

SECTION 2
Faithful

CHAPTER 11

Count the Cost

> "Therefore, since we are surrounded by such a great cloud of witnesses, let us throw off everything that hinders and the sin that so easily entangles. And let us run with perseverance the race marked out for us, fixing our eyes on Jesus, the pioneer and perfecter of faith."
>
> —Hebrews 12:1–2

As we walk through what it means to be faithful, God has taught me over the years that we need to count the cost of every decision we make in life. In Matthew 16:24-25, Jesus shares with the disciples that whoever wants to be his disciple must deny themselves, take up their cross, and follow him. It is important to go into situations with our eyes wide open.

A balance to this is understanding that we perform for an audience of one. If we say we are Christ-followers, then the only audience we perform for is God. He wants us to count the cost as we move forward with our lives, dreams, and plans.

Surrender, Sacrifice, and Success

It's essential to understand that success requires surrender and sacrifice, and we need to focus on what truly matters. Take marriage, for example. Many people believe it's 50/50—if both partners do their half, things will work out. However, that's not true. It needs to be 100/100. Both partners need to be fully committed, giving 100 percent.

If I sit back and say, "I cleaned the kitchen the last two nights, so it's not my turn," it probably won't get done. However, if I take care of it, my husband will contribute in other ways. If we're both working at 100 percent, things get done. It works because we are both fully committed, not just halfway.

This principle of sacrifice and commitment is important in all relationships. In our marriage, we have often chosen to pursue things together, even when we could have done things separately. Starting Anchor Point, for example, required sacrifice on both our parts. We knew it would take time away from our relationship and family, but we believed it was worth it.

When we decided to adopt children from hard backgrounds, we knew there would be challenges, although I'm not sure we fully understood them at the time. But we were committed from day one. I remember one of my children's biological mothers had a diagnosis of bipolar disorder, and they told me the child might also be bipolar.

Bipolar disorder is difficult to diagnose in a young child, and I wondered if she was acting out of her woundedness rather than a mental health issue. Regardless, I was already committed to this child, and no diagnosis was going to change that. I told the judge, "You need to understand that I am already this child's mother, and you are keeping her from me. This is my child."

We entered the adoption process with our eyes wide open, knowing there would be unique challenges. But we trusted that God was calling us to this and that He would see us through. Have we faced hard times with our children? Yes, more than I can count. But we've also had incredible highs.

If my husband and I hadn't stayed committed to walking through our children's trauma and recovery, who else would? It has required great personal sacrifice, but being Jesus' hands and feet to our children as they navigate their challenges is an honor.

I remember one of my children was on the streets, doing drugs, and there were times I didn't know if she was alive. She would send us random text messages with pictures of herself on the street. While most people would find that tragic, I found comfort in knowing she was alive. It's moments like those when being faithful and counting the cost is so important.

The same principle applies in business. When we started Anchor Point, we knew it would be challenging. I also sat down with my children and asked them to consider the cost of adopting more kids. I asked them, "What if I can't pay for your college or buy your car? What if I can't pay for your insurance or your wedding?" They said it would be okay if it meant adopting more children, and I was so proud of them.

Life is about sacrifice, and we need to go into things with our eyes wide open. But if God is calling us to something, we can trust Him to see us through. Whether in family, business, or personal life, we perform for an audience of one. Humility and surrender are key. Success, in God's eyes, is not always what the world sees as success.

There have been times when I have faced difficult decisions, like parting ways with someone in the company. In those moments, I always ask myself if I have done everything I could to help that person succeed, though I know I may not always get it right, and that can be paralyzing. My prayer is that God gives me wisdom, and I trust that He is working redemptively, bringing good to everything and everyone, even in the midst of the unknowns. Ultimately, my deepest desire is to please my Heavenly Father.

That mindset allows me to remain steadfast and faithful, no matter the challenges. Whether things are going well or not, I know I am seeking to walk the path God has set before me, and that gives me peace.

> "God is more concerned about our character than our comfort. His goal is not to pamper us physically, but to perfect us spiritually."
>
> —Paul W. Powell

> "You have to fight to reach your dream. You have to sacrifice and work hard for it."
>
> —Lionel Messi

> "The lasting value of a person's life is measured by the way they live and the legacy they leave for others to follow."
>
> —John C. Maxwell

Make it Personal

1. What decisions in your life required you to count the cost, and what did you learn?

2. How do you weigh the cost of a big decision, and what factors do you consider?

3. What sacrifices are you willing to make to fulfill your purpose, and how do you stay motivated?

4. What step can you take this week to live out the core message of this chapter and inspire others by example?

5. How can embracing this chapter's theme of counting the cost help you make a difference in your community or in someone else's life?

CHAPTER 12

Believe the Best

"Finally, brothers and sisters, whatever is true, whatever is noble, whatever is right, whatever is pure, whatever is lovely, whatever is admirable—if anything is excellent or praiseworthy—think about such things."

—Philippians 4:8

As we continue the journey, one steadfast principle that I have been striving to incorporate into my life is choosing to believe the best in people and situations, no matter how bad things might seem. I see this modeled in the way Jesus saw people when they were not at their best, like Peter's denial in John 21 or the woman caught in adultery in John 8. Jesus looked beyond the situation and loved people, wanting them to be truly free even when they hurt or betrayed Him, and He called out their best. I truly believe that Jesus saw people not just as they were in weak moments but also at their best and who they could be through the transforming power of God's grace.

This has become a foundation for me. I want others to believe the best in me and who I can be in Christ, so I strive to believe the same in them, regardless of the circumstances. A key aspect of this is trust, which is essential in developing strong relationships. In the same way, faithfulness calls us to remain committed to others, reflecting the faithfulness of Christ toward us. Just as Jesus entrusts us with His grace and sees our potential through God's transforming power, we are called to extend that same grace and trust to others. By doing so, we demonstrate the fruit of the Spirit—faithfulness (*Galatians 5:22–23*)—and build relationships that mirror God's enduring love.

Trust

I believe trust is given, not earned. When someone trusts me, I do everything in my power to maintain that trust. I am cautious about under-promising and over-delivering and aim at over-communicating to make sure nothing is left to guesswork. This applies to all areas of life, including my relationship with my husband. Our marriage is built on trust, and I trust him completely. He may not always like the things I need to process as a CEO, and he doesn't always say easy things, but I know he is for me. He has my best interest at heart, and I trust that. He believes in my best and what Christ is doing in me despite my moments of weakness.

We don't turn a blind eye, and there are consequences to actions, but with our children, we choose to trust them. Jesus chooses to trust us (you could call that grace), so we extend that same trust to them. Do they screw up? Yes. Do they lie sometimes? Yes. However, we still choose to trust them. Not because they are always the best decision-makers but because they need to know we are for them and call out their best. They need to feel safe and know that trust is a given in our home.

I've had plenty of experiences where this trust was tested. For example, one of my children smoked marijuana in the house, breaking several rules. She didn't tell the truth at first, but eventually she did. Instead of focusing solely on punishment, I wanted to understand why she did it and why she chose to do it in our home. I realized she might have needed to be caught. We worked through it, and she was likely surprised that we trusted her again, but we did. We trust because it opens the opportunity for growth and reconciliation.

I know that not everything people do comes from good intentions, and some might even be harmful. However, I have learned that believing the best in people and situations helps me maintain the right mental and emotional framework. It allows me to have the mindset of Jesus, to be gracious, and to hold people accountable when necessary.

When there are conflicts with clients, employees, or volunteers, I always strive to believe the best in them. I want to understand what's going on behind the scenes and what's driving the behavior. By getting to the truth, we can move forward.

I remember an early situation with one of my staff members who had been with me for a long time. Something went wrong, and she was upset. I told her, "Stay right there. I'm on my way back to the office, and we're going to talk it through." I reassured her that I believed the best in her and that there must be a reason behind her reaction. We figured it out together because most conflicts arise from miscommunication or assumptions.

If I react poorly to someone's behavior, I risk breaking trust. I have done it and know the damage that can be done. But if I stay present, dig deeper, and seek to understand, I can help resolve the issue while maintaining trust.

Looking Behind Behavior

One strategy that has served me well, whether in my personal life, family, or business, is to always look at what's going on behind the behavior. If we can get to the root of the issue, we can usually find clarity and a way forward. This applies to my relationships with my husband, friends, and colleagues. We don't always agree, but hopefully, we have a trusting relationship where we can speak honestly. Sometimes, we might preface difficult conversations with, "I need you to hear this with grace," or "I'm telling you this because I love you."

Even when it's hard, I trust that God will show me the truth. When I take difficult feedback to Him, I ask for wisdom and clarity. He helps me see whether there's something I need to learn or change or if there's a larger issue at play.

Building strong relationships requires the ability to accept feedback without letting emotions take over. I've learned with much practice to trust God in these situations, allowing Him to reveal what I need to address.

This approach also applies to my children. Many of them come from trauma backgrounds, and they may react strongly to small issues. I remind myself that they are good, precious children in those moments. I try to come alongside them, asking, "What's going on? How can I help?" This approach fosters trust and helps us move forward together.

The same goes for business. To resolve issues effectively, I must be willing to stay in messy situations and work through them. For that to happen, I must be healthy. If I have unresolved trauma or rejection, those situations might trigger me, and I could escalate the problem. When I ask God to reveal areas of woundedness, He helps me heal so I can respond in a healthy way.

God doesn't want us to hold onto hurt. He wants us to bring those wounds to Him so He can heal them, and that often requires the understanding to look underneath and address the root. When we do that, we become the people He needs us to be—for our families, our businesses, and our communities. We become reflections of Jesus.

> "People are often unreasonable and self-centered. Forgive them anyway. If you are kind, people may accuse you of ulterior motives. Be kind anyway. If you are honest, people may cheat you. Be honest anyway. In the end, it is between you and God. It was never between you and them anyway."
>
> —Mother Teresa

> "When we really love someone, we see all the potential they have within them, even if they don't see it themselves."
>
> —Shannon L. Alder

> "Character is the legacy we leave when we're gone and the testament of our faith to the world."
>
> —Anonymous

Make it Personal

1. How do you practice seeing the best in others, especially when they disappoint you?

2. Reflect on a situation where someone believed in you. How did that affect you, and how can you offer the same to others?

3. What steps could you take to nurture a more positive, hopeful outlook toward others?

4. What step can you take this week to live out the core message of this chapter and inspire others by example?

5. How can embracing this chapter's theme of believing the best help you make a difference in your community or in someone else's life?

CHAPTER 13

Dream Big!

"Then the Lord replied: 'Write down the revelation and make it plain on tablets so that a herald may run with it. For the revelation awaits an appointed time; it speaks of the end and will not prove false. Though it linger, wait for it; it will certainly come and will not delay.'"
—Habakkuk 2:2–3

Another important aspect of being faithful is learning to dream big dreams—dreams bigger than we can accomplish on our own. In Ephesians 3:20-21, God says He "is able to do immeasurably more than we can ask or imagine." I have always been captivated by that idea: God wants to do great things in each of us. He wants to work in my life, in your life, in my family, and through our work.

Keep the Faith

We often fear to dream big because we fear the cost. And yes, it may come at a price. But big dreams are worth pursuing.

These are the goals that matter in the end. Who does not want their life to count for something greater than they could have ever imagined? God offers us that opportunity. He doesn't need us to have all the answers or see how we'll get from point A to point B. He just needs us to be faithful and take the next best step, trusting Him to lead and guide us.

That has been a significant theme in my life over the years. When I think about dreaming big, I ask myself, "How do we find faith in difficult times? How do we lean on that faith?"

One of the big dreams God gave me was to have a large family and to be a young grandmother. We set out on that journey, taking one step at a time. After getting pregnant with twins, we found out we were expecting quadruplets. Sadly, they passed away in our arms. At that point, the dream of a large family seemed lost.

However, the truth is, it wasn't. God was looking for us to put a stake in the ground and say, "We will trust you." Even though it didn't feel good at the time, there was no other choice. Where else could we go? Who could we depend on more than Him? So, we trusted that if God had given us a dream for a big family, He would show us how to make it happen. We continued to walk in faith and eventually revisited the idea of trying to have more children.

As the story unfolded, we adopted—not once but three times.

The amazing thing is that our quads—Zach, Josh, Nate, and Chris—were born on April 1, 1995, and that's the day they passed away. Seven years later, on April 1, 2002, our first five children came into our home. God didn't just give us four children; He gave us five. They were not replacements for our lost boys, and I look forward to spending eternity with Zach, Josh, Nate, and Chris. But these children were a blessing beyond what we could have imagined. Since then, we've been blessed with more children and grandchildren in ways we never expected.

I remember sitting in the hospital after losing our boys and telling God, "I'm going to trust You. You've been faithful before, and You'll be faithful again. I know You're writing a good story." My children have taught me many things—how to stretch and grow, how resilient kids can be despite the horrors they've experienced, and how they can still love, trust, and grow. Their stories are part of God's work, and they can reach people I never could because they allow God to use their experiences.

When we started Anchor Point, we put a big dream on paper without really knowing what we were doing. It was just me and another woman praying and asking God, "Is this what You want to do?" We watched Him open doors as we learned to depend on Him. He opened some doors and closed others—and that's okay. We have to trust His process. When I look back at that original plan, I can see everything slowly coming to fruition. It's not finished yet, but we're getting there by being faithful and continuing to move forward step by step.

Look to God First

So, how do you dream big dreams? It means asking God questions like, "What am I uniquely here for? Why have You put me here? What do You want to accomplish through me? How do You want me to be a difference-maker in this world? Show me what you are doing so I can join You." Asking those kinds of questions pleases God. He begins planting seeds in our hearts. For example, God planted a seed of adoption in my life when my parents first talked to me about being pro-life and adopting a child who was abused or abandoned. Little did I know that seed would bear fruit years later.

At Anchor Point, we wrote down our dreams, even though we didn't know what we were doing. But we knew the One who did. We prayed and asked God to guide us and show us the next best step. We committed to shifting or adjusting as needed to align with His vision. Not everything went according to our original plan—like the school that wasn't part of the dream but became part of the story for a while. It taught us valuable lessons and allowed us to help another ministry grow.

Big dreams don't come easy. They bring obstacles. When our dreams align with God's will, Satan will try to sabotage them. That's why we need to be prayed up, ready, and aware that nothing surprises God. We also shouldn't be surprised when challenges arise because anything worth having is worth fighting for—whether it's a marriage, a relationship with our kids, or the next big thing at Anchor Point.

When we are moving in the right direction, communication breakdowns often happen. Satan tries to create division and strife, especially within our team. We have to fight hard to stay united, to talk things through, and to ensure everyone is on the same page. Clear communication is critical to weathering the storms and achieving our big dreams.

Ultimately, for us to dream big dreams, we must depend entirely on God. Big dreams are those we can't accomplish on our own. I don't know how to make a marriage work most of the time. I don't know how to be the perfect mom or run a business. But God does. When we are humble enough to ask Him for help, He guides us. Only through dependence on Him can we accomplish great things and be part of His story.

In the Bible, Paul is a great example. He had big aspirations, but God realigned them. Paul surrendered and became part of something bigger than himself—spreading the Gospel. His faithfulness has impacted generations through his writings in the Bible. The disciples also lived out big dreams, which God used for His glory.

So, dream big dreams. Don't be afraid to go after what God has placed on your heart. When you align your dreams with His, you can't go wrong.

"Dream big because God has big plans for you."
—Chris Tomlin

"God's plans for your life far exceed the circumstances of your day."
—Louie Giglio

"To achieve something you have never achieved before, you must become someone you have never been."
—Les Brown

Make it Personal

1. What big dreams has God placed on your heart? How are you working toward them?

2. How do you approach obstacles to your dreams, and what helps you keep believing?

3. What steps can you take to expand your vision and take bold, faithful steps toward it?

4. What step can you take this week to live out the core message of this chapter and inspire others by example?

5. How can embracing this chapter's theme of dreaming big help you make a difference in your community or in someone else's life?

CHAPTER 14

Find Joy in the Journey

"May the God of hope fill you with all joy and peace as you trust in him, so that you may overflow with hope by the power of the Holy Spirit."

—Romans 15:13

When I think about being faithful, it means being consistent, steadfast, and reliable. While spiritual faithfulness is incredibly important and needs to undergird everything I do, being faithful in a broader sense—being someone who can be counted on—is crucial as we go through life's journey.

Being faithful also means remembering to count the cost because there is always a cost to faithfulness. It involves believing the best in people, dreaming big, and finding joy in the journey.

Embrace the Whole Journey

Here's the deal: The journey God has me on—whether as an individual, a family member, or a business leader—is not made up entirely of highs. It's a mix of highs and lows. I must remember to stay true throughout the process and learn to fall in love with the journey.

By embracing the journey, I can find joy. This means being a person of integrity, ensuring my actions align with my personal values. For me, Jesus is at the center of everything—personal life, family, and business. It is His story I am part of, and I am on this journey with Him.

On this journey, God stretches and grows me because He is deeply invested in who I am becoming as a person. As I grow in my relationship with Him, the goal is to reflect Jesus more and more to those around me in both personal and business matters.

I want that more than anything—to reflect Jesus to others. I know I can't do that alone. It requires the Holy Spirit to work through me. And it takes having people around me who are walking the same path and willing to speak life into me through community. And when I willingly surrender to Him and walk in humility, He stretches and grows me. And interestingly, He often does this by taking me through challenging situations.

So, I would caution you. Unless you are ready to grow, consider carefully before praying and asking God, "What do I need to do to grow more God?" because I trust that is a prayer He is going to answer. He's going to show you, and you'll be given opportunities to learn. God is not interested in letting us stay where we are. He continually challenges us to become more and more like Him, reflecting His image to the world.

How do I put things into the right perspective when things come into my life? My staff has often commented that nothing seems to faze me. I'm usually calm, saying, "It's okay, no worries, God's got this." When they ask, "How are we going to get through this?" I'll respond, "I don't know, but God's got it. We'll pray and trust, and He will reveal the next best step." The goal would be this response every time and I'm working on that.

Even in hard times, we can still experience joy and peace. That's only possible because Jesus *is* peace and joy; I can hold on to that throughout life's journey. The highs are great and fun, but during the challenges that make me want to quit or stay in bed with the covers pulled over my head, I know He is there and everything I need and desire in this life.

However, it's only as I go through these challenges, being honest with Him, humble, and surrendering, that true joy comes. Other ways to maintain joy include living a life of integrity and honesty. In our family, we teach our children how to navigate life when it's not easy and how to be honest and live with integrity, even when it would be easier to turn away or cut corners.

Our kids watch us when we model integrity, but do we also celebrate when they do the hard things? Do we acknowledge when a child finds money in a store and turns it in to the manager instead of keeping it? Or when they find a wallet? Or when they come to you and say, "Mom, I made a bad decision," or "Mom, I broke this"?

Learning these values in small moments is crucial as they move into adulthood. I've found that the ages between eighteen and twenty-six are the hardest because life often treats them harshly, and I can no longer protect them. It is essential to teach them how to walk with integrity and live out values based on how God wants us to live.

Integrity

In business, maintaining integrity is imperative. There should be nothing we do in secret that can't be openly discussed. We protect people, but we don't hide behind things. Integrity means underpromising and overdelivering. When we say something, we follow through—time and time again. It's hard to build trust, and it's very easy to lose it. So, we strive to be trustworthy and ensure people can count on us to do what we promised.

When my actions match my values, life feels right, and there's joy in the journey. When my actions don't align with my values, that's when I feel dissatisfied, distracted, or outside of God's will. I know that when God guides me, and I live according to His word—the Bible— I can find joy and peace because I am in alignment with my Father's will.

When I don't, life is a struggle. Peace and joy come when my actions align with the values He has given me. I can think of many times when that's true, like recently when I was binge-watching a TV show and felt convicted because I hadn't done the things I needed to do.

I needed to accomplish some scripture memorization that I had committed to. Yet, I found myself binge-watching a TV show. It wasn't a bad show, but I questioned whether it would have been better for me to focus on hiding God's word in my heart.

I felt a strong conviction about this. Watching the show wasn't bringing me any real joy, so I decided to make a change. I committed to turning off the TV and ensuring my scripture memorization or Bible reading was up to date every time I felt the urge to watch. At first, there were moments of frustration. I thought, *If I had just done this earlier, I could have watched that show.* But I had to choose to bring my actions into alignment with my beliefs.

I can honestly say it has been incredibly beneficial. Scripture memorization and Bible reading have greatly impacted my life, bringing more joy, purpose, and guidance than any TV show ever could. I experience joy, peace, and a sense of purpose when I prioritize these things. That's what I need to desire more than the fleeting satisfaction of sitting mindlessly in front of the TV.

This is how I find joy—by making sure my actions reflect my values. For my family and my kids, we've always planted positive seeds, left them a bridge to Jesus, and taught them that they will never truly be happy until they learn to love themselves as Jesus loves them and fall in love with Him along the journey.

Faith in Action

As we discussed earlier, when my daughter was on the streets as a prostitute, and another was struggling with drug addiction, they were both absolutely miserable. The lives they were leading were full of chaos. However, as they began making better decisions and moving toward positive progress, we saw joy and peace come into their lives. As my children have come to know God better and follow Him more closely, we've seen an increase in peace in their lives. Do they still have a long way to go? Sure. And so do I. But I believe we can all learn to walk through our struggles together.

One family experience involved my daughter saying something at school after a test where she got a bad grade. She was extremely distraught and told a friend, "My dad's going to kill me." Her teacher overheard this but didn't hear the rest of the conversation.

When my daughter's friend reassured her that her dad wouldn't actually kill her, our daughter clarified that dad was not going to be happy. Unfortunately, the teacher missed this part, and the next day, she asked my daughter some questions and, out of concern, reported the situation to Child Protective Services (CPS).

Having CPS open an investigation into the safety of my child and accusing my husband of wrongdoing was not part of our plans for the week. Of course, none of the accusations were true, but the words of a child were blown out of proportion. We understood the teacher's concern for my daughter's safety, but it was still difficult.

When CPS becomes involved in your life, you have a few choices. You can freak out—which, admittedly, we did a little—or you can recognize that God is not surprised by the situation. One of my biggest concerns was that my other children wouldn't blame or take it out on the daughter involved, but instead, we would walk through this together as a family. We hired an attorney, and I spoke with my daughter that evening.

I said, "I hear there was some excitement at school. Tell me what happened." She explained, and I said, "Well, CPS called, and they're going to come check us out because some people misunderstood what you said and think something bad has happened." Then, I explained it to her in terms she could understand, using an analogy about exaggeration: "It's like if you told someone that mom 'pigged out' on ice cream. What would they think?" My kids replied that people would assume I ate a lot. I explained, "But in reality, I ate just four little spoons before I felt sick. People don't understand that when you say 'pigged out,' you mean only a few bites. So, we have to be careful with our words."

After that, we gathered as a family and discussed how we would walk through this together. We talked about the importance of always telling the truth as well as words and their power. Then, we turned on some worship music, praised God, and prayed. We asked God to show us the way through. The process ran its course, and all was well, but it was also an opportunity to grow as a family. This is how we build resilience as a family: by walking through difficult situations together and learning to trust in God.

When my job at Prison Fellowship ended, we had a "what's next" party to look forward to the doors God would open for the future. It taught my kids that things don't always go as planned but that we can trust God to guide us.

The same approach has applied to my work. Whether it's facing a lawsuit, a financial shortfall, or any other challenge, stopping to ensure my staff is okay, praising God, and trusting in His guidance has always been our approach. We've had years when money was tight, and we had to get creative with spending. But every time, we trusted that God was in control.

These themes—trusting God, finding joy in the journey, and being faithful—have played out in my personal life, family life, and business. No matter the circumstances, I know God is in control. I know He is not surprised by anything. Whether the journey feels good or challenging, He is with me, guiding and leading the way, just as He has promised.

It is in the lowest moments of life that I have felt closest to Him—whether it was losing my boys, which ultimately led to starting Anchor Point or facing other difficulties. It's in those lows that I've needed Him the most, and that's when I've experienced His presence most deeply.

Staying in that "sweet space" of relying on God allows me to reflect Him to others. When people see that, they are drawn to ask what makes the difference. And I get to tell them that it is God who makes all the difference in this journey.

"Joy is the serious business of Heaven."

—C.S. Lewis

"You have as much laughter as you have faith."

—Martin Luther

"The journey is the reward."

—Chinese Proverb

Make it Personal

1. In what ways do you find joy even when things don't go as planned?

2. How do you intentionally cultivate joy, and how does it impact your life?

3. Reflect on a time when you felt joy despite challenges. What made that possible?

4. What step can you take this week to live out the core message of this chapter and inspire others by example?

5. How can embracing this chapter's theme of finding joy in the journey help you make a difference in your community or in someone else's life?

SECTION 3
Fearless

CHAPTER 15

Be Committed and Steadfast

"Therefore, my dear brothers and sisters, stand firm. Let nothing move you. Always give yourselves fully to the work of the Lord, because you know that your labor in the Lord is not in vain."

—1 Corinthians 15:58

We are moving into the final section on being fearless. Being fearless doesn't mean the absence of fear—everyone has fears—but it's about being willing to face those fears despite feeling them.

Another aspect of being fearless is shifting my focus from fearing what the world and people around me think to revering what God thinks. When I stand in awe of God, I become willing to do whatever it takes to follow Him faithfully. Over the years, I have learned to cultivate fearlessness by staying committed and steadfast, overcoming challenges, and moving from merely surviving to truly thriving. This trust in God works both ways: as we grow fearless through trusting Him, we also learn to remain steadfast and calm, even when life feels out of control. In facing daily obstacles, this trust helps us build resilience and perseverance, strengthening our faith with each step forward.

Being fearless also means being willing to jump in and do the hard things necessary to reach the next level. We will talk about that a little later, but first, let's look closer at what it means to be steadfast.

Be Steadfast, Stay Calm

One of my former staff members recently shared a testimony about me, and although she hasn't worked for me in quite some time, her words fit this section of the book perfectly. She mentioned that over the years, she had observed me in various aspects of life—whether in my personal life, with my children, in business, in large groups or small, and during both good and challenging times.

She said she had seen me navigate all these situations, and, to her, the one consistent trait she noticed was that I was always calm, regardless of the circumstances. She kindly added that in all the time she worked with me, she couldn't recall a moment when I seemed rattled or even needed to take a break; I was able to remain present and continue in difficult situations.

Her words were gracious, and while I certainly don't get it right all the time, it's wonderful to hear someone describe me as a calm, steadfast person in the face of both highs and lows.

When we talk about being committed, steadfast, and calm, even when everything and everyone around us seems out of control, I often say, "No worries." If we have God as the center of our lives, businesses, families—everything—then we truly have no worries. Nothing we face is a surprise to Him.

Though it may catch me off guard, I trust that He is writing a good story for my life, my children, our business, and our ministry and that He is working all things for my good.

He always has my best interests at heart, even when I may not feel it in the moment. I can remain calm because I've learned to trust that. I can be fully present in every situation I face, seeking to understand what's happening behind the scenes rather than reacting emotionally.

It's encouraging that my staff sees this quality in me, and I aspire to always maintain it. My children, however, would likely tell you that I've had my moments of losing my temper as a mom. However, even that is not entirely negative, as it presents an opportunity to teach resilience and recovery. It also gives me the chance to humble myself and apologize, which is important for them to see—that adults aren't perfect, but we are growing, too.

I would say that, as a mom, God has supernaturally granted me the ability to stay calm during the big crises of life. Whether it was CPS visiting our home, children living on the streets making poor decisions, engaging in inappropriate relationships, or finding themselves in abusive situations, I remained steadfast. Whether it was receiving troubling calls from school about bad decisions or even visiting a child in jail, I wanted my children to know that I am for them and there for them. No matter what the world throws their way or what they manage to get themselves into, I will be calm and steadfast and help them face their fears and find their way forward.

God has used calmness and steadfastness in my life and I look to Jesus's journey to the cross as the ultimate example of calm and steadfastness. He endured terrible suffering for us but remained focused on His goal and purpose. He knew the price He had to pay and walked through it willingly.

Take Calculated Risks with Faith

Along with steadfastness, there is also the aspect of being fearless that can allow risk taking where fear would stop others. Calculated (cost-counted) risk-taking to venture down paths others would avoid. I am not referring to recklessness but the willingness to follow God despite what we see as dangers and risks. Missionaries often move forward with this form of fearless trust in God.

I remember a time when I had a goal to take better care of my body. I started walking, but walking alone wasn't enough; I needed a big goal, something to strive for. So, I set out to complete a marathon. It required a lot of training, especially since I was quite heavy at the time. This big goal ran the risk of failure and disappointment. But I successfully accomplished that goal. Afterward, I did another marathon. Then, I found the Half Marathon Challenge, which required completing ten half marathons in a year, and I set out to achieve that goal.

I discovered that once you successfully take a risk, it becomes easier to take the next one. Completing each half marathon became easier, as I could stretch myself while my body was still in shape, rather than taking a break and working my way back to the same fitness level. This principle of balancing risk and wisdom has been invaluable to me, not just physically, but in my personal life, family, and business. I learned that I could grow faster if I continued to push forward, with God's guidance, rather than stopping and taking it easy for too long.

Adopting children from hard backgrounds was one of our biggest calculated risks. We knew they would bring complexities into our lives, but we were confident God was leading us in that direction and trusted Him to help us find our way. I remember when we first started looking into adoption. My dad saw a boy and a girl on a website and said, "One boy and one girl would be perfect." But I replied, "Dad, I want four kids," and he thought I was crazy. But I felt strongly that I was supposed to have four children. Little did I know it would ultimately be nine children.

As we ventured down that road, many people told us we were making a mistake, that adopting five children was too much. But we did it anyway. It was complicated and had its highs and lows, but it was worth it. Those children brought both challenges and tremendous joy to our lives.

When we went to adopt for the second time, my parents were completely against it. They thought having five children already was overwhelming, and they refused to be a reference for us. I believe they did this out of love and concern, but it was still a shock that my own parents wouldn't support me in this way, especially since I consider myself a good mom. Then, I called my brother, and he said he didn't want to get between me and Dad, so he also refused to be a reference.

I had to move forward with the adoption without any of my family acting as references, which felt strange, but we found others who were willing to vouch for us. When we adopted the second set of children, my parents were surprised. They had grown to love the first five but didn't quite know how to react to the next two. Over time, they warmed up to the idea, but it certainly brought more complexities into our lives—both in good ways and challenging ones. Yet, God was faithful through it all. The second time we adopted, our kids were completely on board, but I don't think they fully understood how difficult it might be. It was a growth opportunity for all of us.

When we felt called to adopt for the third time, the kids were definitely more involved. They helped us narrow down the children we applied for. We didn't even tell my parents or brother we were considering another adoption until the process was well underway. I called my parents only when the children were about to move into our home. When I told them, my mom simply said, "That sounds exactly like you." This experience taught me that along life's journey, there will always be people—family included—who will say, "This isn't a good idea," or "This isn't a good risk to take." It's important to listen to them, but following what God calls us to do is far more important.

Even my pastor expressed concerns about our third adoption, asking, "Are you sure this is a good idea?" I remember thinking, *You're my pastor—you're supposed to encourage me to follow God's call.* But that's okay. You have to know who your audience of one is. You have to be confident in your calling. If God calls you to do something, it's not a risk. It may be hard and challenging, but it's not a risk. And you have to fear God more than you fear what people around you think or say.

In business, very few people thought starting a nonprofit was a good idea. Most believed it would be too hard; I even thought it sounded difficult. In the early days of starting our nonprofit, most people would say things like, "That sounds great. Let me know how it goes." It wasn't until about three years after we had moved beyond the startup phase that people began to take us seriously and become more committed to the cause.

So, when you venture into a new business or ministry that God has called you to, many will say it can't be done or that it's too hard. You have to know your why—why you're called to this purpose—and be confident in it. I suggest writing it down, putting it somewhere you can see, and constantly reminding yourself of God's promise or the passion He has ignited in you. Trust that as you take the next best steps, He will guide, mold, and, if needed, change them to bring you to the right place.

I would venture to say that as we have grown with Anchor Point and expanded by adding the maternity home, the medical clinic, and various community initiatives, each step has involved due diligence, prayer, and a willingness to walk the path God has laid before us. Along the way, God has opened and closed doors.

There have been aspects of Anchor Point where we started something, but it didn't work out. In those cases, we made the hard decision to stop what wasn't working. These decisions are never easy, especially when people are attached to certain initiatives or when there is a desire to do everything. However, sometimes, we must acknowledge where God is leading, and difficult choices must be made.

When we take on new ventures, we must understand who we perform for—we perform for God, not for the approval of those around us. This perspective helps us face uncertainty and take calculated risks. Uncertainty can arise when things try to knock us off center, confuse us, or even derail our progress. For example, when my child makes a poor decision that reflects badly on me as a mom or when a business colleague acts in a way that is destructive to the team or to me personally, it can create doubt about whether I'm doing the right thing, or whether I'm a failure as a leader or a parent.

In these moments, I have to remind myself of God's calling, how I am to live that out, and how I must continue moving forward. Uncertainty may be surprising to me, but it is never a surprise to Him. He will guide me through it. Often, these uncertain times reveal areas of weakness—whether it's personal healing I need or growth in my leadership skills. These lessons help me become stronger for the future.

By remaining committed and steadfast, I can face my fears and remain fearless in the face of those around me and the challenges that come my way.

"Faithfulness is not doing something right once but doing something right over and over and over and over."

—Joyce Meyer

"The only limit to our realization of tomorrow will be our doubts of today."

—Franklin D. Roosevelt

"Commitment is an act, not a word."

—Jean-Paul Sartre

Make it Personal

1. How has God used adversity in your life to shape your character and faith?

2. Describe a situation where trusting God was difficult. What helped you persevere?

3. How do you stay hopeful and resilient when facing adversity?

4. What step can you take this week to live out the core message of this chapter and inspire others by example?

5. How can embracing this chapter's theme of trusting God through adversity help you make a difference in your community or in someone else's life?

CHAPTER 16

Overcomer — Survive to Thrive

"When you pass through the waters, I will be with you, and when you pass through the rivers, they will not sweep over you. When you walk through the fire, you will not be burned; the flames will not set you ablaze."

—Isaiah 43:2

Another key aspect of learning to be fearless as we grow is overcoming the fears we face and the need to build self-confidence. This self-assurance allows us to enter difficult situations with our heads held high, knowing who we are and how we can navigate challenges.

Confronting Fear

Throughout my life, there have been numerous times when I've had to confront and overcome fear. One experience that stands out is my struggle with infertility. During that time, I battled fears of failure, of not being a good spouse or wife, and I felt a deep blow to my self-confidence as a woman.

The inability to have children made me feel defective and I remember the overwhelming desire not to be defined by this struggle.

My husband, like many men, wanted to fix the situation. While his intentions were good, his efforts often made me feel worse. In moments like these, when we feel down and out, unable to see a way through or to overcome, fear can take hold. It makes us feel less than, as though we will never be enough.

This is when I often sense the work of Satan, trying to influence my mind and thoughts, keeping me from becoming the person I've been called to be. What I've found in these moments is that overcoming these fears and negative thoughts is crucial to moving forward in life.

Another story is when we finally became pregnant and found out we were expecting quadruplets. We did everything we could to ensure the boys would arrive safely, but then I was involved in a car accident. My water broke, and I found myself in the hospital, completely powerless to change the situation.

Being in a situation where I have no control is completely unnerving. There was nothing I could do but be in the moment and let God guide me through it. It was a time when I felt stuck and helpless.

When the boys were born, and I held them as they passed away, it was a surreal experience. Holding someone you love deeply, knowing they are leaving you and going to heaven, is indescribable. It can either leave you stuck for the rest of your life, or you somehow find a way to move forward.

Then there was the time my child called to tell me she was a prostitute on the streets. She tried to brush it off as if it were no big deal, but I knew otherwise. Or when my son walked into the room and said, "I'd rather be hanging out with my girlfriend than being here," essentially telling us, "I love you guys, but I'm out of here," before walking out and abandoning his family—leaving his brothers and sisters in distress.

Those were hard times. When CPS came knocking because of something a child said at school, or when a daughter fell in love with drugs and unstable relationships, living on the streets in abject poverty because of her choices. Or when another child ended up pregnant outside of marriage, overwhelmed by her situation, struggling with the decision of whether or not to choose life for her child. When I watched my grandmother, my Nanny, die of multiple sclerosis, I felt helpless. The list goes on and on. We all face these moments.

In business, I have had times when I thought I was doing my best, only to have an employee respond unfairly. There was an employee we dealt with the right way, yet she left and sued the company. I've had expansion efforts thwarted. I've had people spread false information to donors or board members. The list of challenges continues—things that make you feel overwhelmed, fearful, and unsure of how to move forward, with life pressing in on you and stress becoming unbearable.

There are health issues, too, like when I accidentally shut the door on my leg, which led to a staph infection that wouldn't heal. The wound doctor couldn't fix it, and my health was declining without a clear solution.

These are all overwhelming situations. However, one thing God has taught me over time is that to figure my way through, with His guidance, I must move from asking *why* I'm in a situation to learning *how* to survive and, ultimately, how to thrive.

When I ask, "Why?" I spend too much time on that question, which doesn't help. In truth, when I get to heaven, the *why* won't matter anymore. There's no answer to the *why* question on this side of heaven that will ever fully satisfy in those hard moments.

There is no answer to losing boys, having a daughter on the streets as a prostitute, a son abandoning the family, or a child ending up in jail. There is no satisfying answer to *why*. The longer I dwell on that question, the more stuck I become.

The sooner I can shift to asking *how I survive and find my way through*, the sooner God can work with that. The reality is, if you look at Job's story in the Bible, God never answers the question of *why*. He never explained to Job why he went through such suffering. In fact, when Job continued to lament and ask why, God essentially said, "I am God—who are you to question me? Do you control the tides? Do you make these things happen?" And Job had to respond, "No." Job, too, had to learn to stop asking, "Why?" and instead ask, "How do I survive?" That's the question God can work with.

In these situations, whether it was dealing with infertility or loss, God opened our hearts to adoption—something we might never have considered if my boys had lived. Would Anchor Point exist? Probably not, at least not because of me, because I would have been busy raising those four boys. God used that painful situation to lead us in a new direction.

How Do I Thrive?

When I lost the boys, God showed me, bit by bit, how to get through each day. Sometimes, it was moving forward in five-minute increments, sometimes thirty minutes or an hour at a time. As I trusted Him, He showed me the way forward and through the challenging situation. As I moved forward, I didn't want to get stuck in bitterness. I wanted to get better. So, I began to ask, "How do I thrive?"

That's when the full surrender came. I gave my pain to God and asked Him to make something beautiful from it, as He promises. When I laid the heartache of not having children at His feet, I trusted that He had a plan for me, that

He had given me a heart to love children, and that He would somehow meet my desire for a family.

I trusted that God would show me how to survive and help me. I often felt lost and overwhelmed when I faced situations with my kids. I didn't know how to help them or get through the challenges we faced. I would find myself asking, "How do we do this?"

I remember when my daughter wanted to buy a car. I didn't think she should. She found a used car at a no-name lot, and one of her brothers thought it was a great deal. I thought they were both crazy. These were young adults, but I still wasn't convinced it was a good idea.

She came back and said she had to pay in cash or with a cashier's check, and I remember thinking, *This is not a good idea.* I told her as much, but it was her money, and she really wanted to go through with it. Ultimately, despite my reservations, she did.

Long story short, she could never get the title for the car. The state eventually shut down the dealership. I was at a loss: How were we going to get the title? Instead of staying stuck on *why*, I started asking, "God, how do we survive this? How do we get through it?"

My daughter brought the information she had, and through a series of divine connections, we discovered that the car was tied to a local credit union. I had a long-standing relationship with the bank and even knew the CEO. I called him and explained our situation, and he graciously agreed to help. His staff worked on it, and we discovered another person was in the same situation with the dealership. He had traded the car that my daughter now had for another car. The man graciously signed the title over, and the bank transferred it to my daughter, clearing everything up.

The car is not a big deal in the grand scheme of things. However, we had no clear way through that situation, so we started walking forward by praying and asking God to show us the next best step. God opened doors for us that we could never have figured out on our own. We were blessed by that resolution and clearly saw God's hand at work.

To move confidently from asking "Why?" to "How do I survive?" to "How do I thrive?" we need a solid relationship with God. We have to trust Him with our stories, knowing that we don't always need an answer to *why* but that we can trust He is writing a good story. He will lead us through each step faithfully.

Our self-confidence doesn't come from within ourselves but from knowing the One who does have all the answers. For me, that has always been God—through my personal life, my family, and my business. Every time I faced something meant to derail me, if I could move past the *why* and ask *how I could survive* and *thrive*, He was faithful in guiding me every step of the way.

> "When a train goes through a tunnel and it gets dark, you don't throw away the ticket and jump off. You sit still and trust the engineer."
> —Corrie Ten Boom

> "Although the world is full of suffering, it is also full of the overcoming of it."
> —Helen Keller

> "Live a life of love, just as Christ loved us and gave himself up for us as a fragrant offering and sacrifice to God."
> —Ephesians 5:2

Make it Personal

1. What past challenges have you not only survived but also grown from?

2. How do you practice resilience and maintain a positive outlook?

3. In what areas of your life do you want to move from surviving to truly thriving?

4. What step can you take this week to live out the core message of this chapter and inspire others by example?

5. How can embracing this chapter's theme of surviving to thriving help you make a difference in your community or in someone else's life?

CHAPTER 17

Resilience and Perseverance

"We are hard pressed on every side, but not crushed; perplexed, but not in despair; persecuted, but not abandoned; struck down, but not destroyed."

—2 Corinthians 4:8–9

To be fearless, you and I must develop great resilience and perseverance. Over the years, I've found that we won't always get it right as we move forward. We will make mistakes, encounter difficulties, and need the ability to bounce back and keep going.

Resilience

Resilience is not built on perfection. It's built when we fail, turn things around, and get back up. In life, relationships, and families, one of the best ways to build resilience is by making mistakes and having loving people come alongside us. They look into our eyes, see our value, and help us repair the relationship so we can move forward.

Resilience is forged through disappointment or disruption, followed by repair, allowing us to continue onward. There's an example I've heard that may need some fact-checking, but the idea is that when a bone breaks and heals, it becomes stronger than it was before. That's the essence of resilience.

I have certainly encountered disagreements in my personal relationships, particularly with my spouse. If you're married, you know that disagreements are inevitable. The key for us has been the willingness to humble ourselves, work through our issues, and repair our relationship. This process has only strengthened our marriage, giving us the resilience needed for family, business, and life.

My closest and best friendships are those where we feel safe enough to confront one another when we mess up. These friends are willing to help you up, confront you with love, and give you the hope and courage to keep going.

Life isn't about avoiding mistakes. With my children, when they've strayed or found themselves in difficult situations, coming alongside them with unconditional love, regardless of their actions or attitudes, has been incredibly powerful in repairing and strengthening our relationships.

I remember when my son told us he'd rather hang out with his girlfriend than be a part of our family. He left and left heartbreak within our family. After she went off to college and his friends left for school, he had about six more months until his military boot camp started. It did not take long before he realized he'd severed ties with his family, leaving him lonely and struggling. I reached out to him, and it was clear he was having a hard time. I could tell he wanted to come home.

I had always told my kids that they couldn't just come back without serious reflection once they left. He admitted that he wanted to return, and I reminded him that he'd burned a lot of bridges and had a lot of repairing to do. He agreed. I explained that if he returned, he'd have to follow the house rules, not as punishment but because it was best for everyone, especially the younger kids still at home. I also told him he'd need to work hard to rebuild his relationships, particularly with his dad and siblings, and earn back their trust as a big brother.

We welcomed him back, and over those six months, he worked diligently to restore his relationships and rebuild the friendships with the siblings he had hurt. By the time he left for the military, he was in a much better place with his family. That experience was powerful for all of us because it showed him that he could count on his family, and he knew we'd be there for him.

While he was away, there were times he called late at night, unsure of what to do. I'd tell him, "It's okay, son, just breathe, and we'll figure this out." Sometimes, he'd make poor decisions, and I'd remind him, "What you're doing doesn't honor God, and until it does, it's going to be hard for you to find your way out." Still, I was always there for him, seeing the precious person he is. God continued to work in his life; today, he's an amazing father. I had the privilege of standing by him during those hard times, seeing his potential, and helping shape him into the man God created him to be.

I see this same need for resilience in staff members who sometimes make poor choices, knowingly or unknowingly. The key is still seeing the good in them and recognizing their value to the team. My husband likes to quote that humility is the soil in which all the other fruits grow. I think this applies to these situations where resilience is learned. Humility helps people find a way through. The ones who push back or blame others tend to leave the organization, and we must be okay with that. Not everyone is ready or at a similar point in their journey. However, those whose focus is humility and surrender to what God is doing in them or around them will develop resilience in the face of adversity – which is powerful.

Perseverance

Persevering through adversity is something I've experienced firsthand. For example, after I injured my leg by shutting the truck door on it, I struggled with a staph infection that wouldn't heal. The wound doctor couldn't figure it out, and they wanted to hospitalize me, but I refused. When I finally found a natural solution, I didn't know if it would work.

However, I stuck with it, seeing gradual improvement, even though some things got worse before getting better. My nutritionist encouraged me, saying, "Stay the course. It may seem bad now, but keep doing the next right thing. This will pass."

At times, I could hardly believe it would get better, but I trusted his wisdom. Over three years, I stayed committed, making good decisions day after day. I certainly made some bad decisions along the way, but my consistent good choices outweighed the bad, and my health improved. Today, I'm free of medication and healthier than I've been in years, both physically and mentally.

This journey required realistic goals, trust in those guiding me, and the discipline to say no to things that weren't good for me. The same principles apply to our walk with God. He's asking us to stay the course, take the next best step, and trust that a lifetime of faithful obedience will lead to transformation. I've always taught my children that hard work pays off and is more valuable than any talent or skill.

Every one of my children knows they don't have to be the valedictorian, but if they work hard, stay committed, and use their words to express their needs, they'll be successful. School has always been a challenge for my kids. I remember one of my sons needed to prepare for a standardized test. I took him out of school for two days, telling him we'd spend that time studying. He wasn't thrilled, but I said, "You can fight me, or you can work with me, but we're going to do this, and you're going to pass." He worked so hard, and in the end, he did pass. It was a lesson in grit and determination.

Most of my kids have completed a half marathon, and a few have even done a full marathon. During the race, they often asked, "How much farther?" I'd tell them, "Just keep putting one foot in front of the other, and we'll get there." When they felt they couldn't go on, I'd encourage them, "Let's just walk for ten more minutes. We can do this." And eventually, we'd cross the finish line.

Having friends and family who come alongside you is essential. People who have already walked the path and are willing to reach back and help you along the way are invaluable. The same applies to business—you'll face difficulties, but perseverance and resilience will see you through.

Whether it is an economic downturn, a COVID crisis, a shortage of materials and goods needed to work with clients, or an ungrateful client who is abusive to my staff, these challenges inevitably arise.

As leaders, our job is to persevere, no matter the circumstances. We take the next best step, do the next right thing, and seek guidance from those who have gone ahead of us. They can help us navigate the situations we find ourselves in and remind us to celebrate the joy in the journey.

I recall when I first faced a lawsuit. I was talking with a donor of Anchor Point, a man who owns multi-million-dollar companies and is familiar with being sued. I told him how overwhelmed I felt and how I couldn't think straight after this lawsuit came my way for the first time. He laughed and said, "It happens all the time. You've made it. When someone sues you, it means you're doing the right things."

While I'm not sure about that logic in all circumstances, his ability to laugh about it struck me, and I wanted to have that same lighthearted perspective. He guided me through the process, for which I am deeply grateful. His wisdom helped me move past the "woe is me" mentality and realize that I could figure my way through it.

With God by my side, leading the way, I knew I could navigate even this.

> "By perseverance the snail reached the ark."
> —Charles Spurgeon

> "Do not judge me by my successes; judge me by how many times I fell down and got back up again."
> —Nelson Mandela

> "What we do in life echoes in eternity."
> —Maximus in *Gladiator*

Make it Personal

1. What do resilience and perseverance mean to you, and how do you apply them?

2. How do you handle setbacks, and what keeps you moving forward?

3. Describe a time when perseverance paid off. What did that teach you about yourself?

4. What step can you take this week to live out the core message of this chapter and inspire others by example?

5. How can embracing this chapter's theme of resilience and perseverance help you make a difference in your community or in someone else's life?

Conclusion
Summing Up the Journey

"I have fought the good fight, I have finished the race, I have kept the faith. Now there is in store for me the crown of righteousness, which the Lord, the righteous Judge, will award to me on that day—and not only to me but also to all who have longed for his appearing."

—2 Timothy 4:7–8

As we journeyed together, I hope you have picked up some key insights from this book—small lessons that, over time, can lead to significant changes. I have been very blessed in my life to have had many opportunities to learn by experience. Some lessons have come repeatedly, but they have allowed me to see where I've grown.

Take note of the keywords or thoughts that truly struck you and lean into them. Many of these ideas may spur you on your journey to building a legacy. Whether you realize it or not, you are living your legacy every day. To build a meaningful one requires us to be focused, faithful, and fearless.

When you are focused, you know your end goal, eliminate distractions, and choose the next best step. To be faithful in your journey means understanding the cost before you begin and knowing that your audience of one is God. Faithfulness calls for trust in His plan, even when the path is unclear.

We must believe the best in situations and people, entering into each moment with a redeeming perspective. We are called to dream big—bigger than anything we can accomplish on our own—and to find joy in the journey. To be fearless, we must stay committed and steadfast, overcoming challenges and embracing resilience.

When we face difficulties, we need to move from asking, "Why?" to asking, "How do I survive?" and ultimately, "How do I thrive?" Building perseverance and resilience allows us to become the fearless leaders God has called us to be.

If you've found concepts in this book that resonated with you, I encourage you to start small. I didn't learn these lessons overnight—it's been a long process of wrestling through them and applying them one step at a time. Start by picking one or two principles and ask God to show you how to apply them in your life. Ask Him to help you become more resilient, to find joy in your journey, and to grow in focus. He will guide you through this process. Wrap these themes around you, understanding that this is how we build our legacy—by being focused, faithful, and fearless. However, these principles only work fully within the context of a deep relationship with Jesus Christ. While we can apply them to some extent on our own, personal growth and transformation happen most profoundly when we are surrendered to Him.

Ultimately, it comes back to my dependence on Him as my Lord and Savior. How humble and surrendered am I to the calling He has given me through the highs and lows? How willing am I to set aside my desires to take up His higher purpose? And what am I willing to sacrifice so that others may come to know Him or experience His blessings?

It's about the journey of becoming the person God wants me to be and who He is cultivating me to become rather than focusing solely on specific actions or accomplishments.

I want you to walk away knowing that each step you take to align yourself with what God is calling you to do is powerful. Over time, those steps will create a world-changing impact as you consistently move in the next best direction.

We will all leave a legacy—there's no doubt about that. Every choice we make, and every action we take contributes to the legacy we're building. The real question is whether we will be intentional about it and whether our legacy will continue to positively impact others after we've left this world, pointing them toward Jesus as their Savior. That's what excites me.

Lastly, as you've read this book, I hope you've gained insight into my journey—the highs and the lows. I wanted to share my experiences authentically, showing the reality of this path we all walk. Life is a journey filled with both triumphs and challenges, and we get to choose our attitude and approach as we navigate through it.

Don't just read this book and set it aside. Let its message settle in your heart. Dare to ask God what He wants you to do, think, and change based on what you've read. I know something resonated with you, encouraging you to pursue life differently. That's what it's all about—learning and growing together, becoming the people God has called us to be, and making the impact He has designed us to make. Every day, we create a legacy in our business or ministry, our family, and our life. May we do it with great joy so that God is ultimately glorified.

"Not only so, but we also glory in our sufferings, because we know that suffering produces perseverance; perseverance, character; and character, hope. And hope does not put us to shame, because God's love has been poured out into our hearts through the Holy Spirit, who has been given to us."

—Romans 5:3–5

"The place God calls you to is the place where your deep gladness and the world's deep hunger meet."

—Frederick Buechner

"Hardships often prepare ordinary people for an extraordinary destiny."

—C.S. Lewis

"To live is to love and leave a legacy that honors God."

—Anonymous

Make it Personal

1. What fears hold you back from being the person you feel called to be?

2. How do you step out in faith, even when facing fear or doubt?

3. What practical steps can you take to grow in courage and live more fearlessly?

4. What step can you take this week to live out the core message of this chapter and inspire others by example?

5. How can embracing this chapter's theme of living fearlessly help you make a difference in your community or in someone else's life?

Acknowledgments

Scott, thank you for your unwavering belief in me, your constant encouragement, and the steadfast support that has fueled my dreams. Thank you for standing beside me every step of the way, putting up with more than most, and loving me unconditionally. It is because of you I can go out and tackle the world.

Michael, Julia, Alex, Stephen, Shelby, Edward, Tanya, Alisia, Jeffery, and all the grandkids! You have been some of my greatest teachers, showing me resilience, joy, and the beauty of growth. God gave me you, and I cannot imagine my life without you. I pray that each of you will be a Kingdom legacy maker in your life, your family, and your work. Thank you for the lessons, laughter, and love that have shaped me in ways beyond measure.

Mom & Dad—Thank you for the foundation of love and integrity you built into my life from the very beginning. Your sacrifices, guidance and unwavering support have shaped me into the person I am today. You taught me the value of hard work, the importance of kindness, and the power of believing in God's purpose for my life. I am forever grateful for the countless ways you have poured into me with wisdom, encouragement and unconditional love. Your legacy lives on in all that I do.

The Anchor Point staff, board, and volunteers—your dedication, compassion, and commitment to our mission inspire me daily. Thank you for your hard work, faithfulness, and heart for serving others. Together, we are making a lasting impact, and I am honored to be on this journey with each of you.

Our many wonderful friends who have prayed for us throughout our lives and on this book-writing journey. You know who you are. I am forever grateful. Your behind-the-scenes work has paved the way for this to become a reality. May God richly bless you in the days and weeks to come.

Appendix

Debbie Simmons

Anchor Point

Transforming Families, Restoring Lives: A Legacy of Faith and Hope

Anchor Point stands as a living testament to the transformative power of faith, love, and hope in action. Located in League City, Texas, this nonprofit organization weaves biblical principles into its mission, serving as a lighthouse for families facing life's toughest storms. At its core is an unshakable belief in the promises of God and a guiding scripture that inspires their every endeavor:

> "We have this hope as an anchor for the soul, firm and secure" (Hebrews 6:19a, NIV).

This verse beautifully encapsulates Anchor Point's mission—to provide a steady, unwavering presence for families, grounded in the hope that only God can give.

Hope for Every Family

Imagine a mother walking into the Hope Family Center, burdened with the weight of life's trials. She's met with compassion and understanding, and through the guidance offered, she begins to feel the love of Christ surrounding her. Here, families are reminded of the promise in Isaiah 41:10, "So do not fear, for I am with you; do not be dismayed, for I am your God. I will strengthen you and help you; I will uphold you with my righteous right hand."

Anchor Point embraces individuals and families where they are, offering counseling, resources, and the encouragement they need to rebuild their lives.

A Sanctuary for Women

At the Obria Medical Clinic, young women are given more than medical care; they're given hope. Imagine a frightened teenager learning she's not alone, as caring hands and hearts reflect the love found in Psalm 139:13-14, "For you created my inmost being; you knit me together in my mother's womb. I praise you because I am fearfully and wonderfully made."

This clinic is a safe place where women can reclaim their dignity and confidence, knowing that they are valued and cherished by the Creator.

Transforming Families Through God's Truth

The Hope Community Initiatives empower parents with tools and wisdom rooted in scripture while raising up the next generation of pro-life leaders. Picture a father, distant from his child, learning how to rebuild trust and connection. Here, families find encouragement in Proverbs 22:6, "Start children off on the way they should go, and even when they are old, they will not turn from it."

Many women have seen their lives radically changed and experienced healing from past abortions, sexual abuse, or trauma through one of our many recovery groups.

Through practical training and spiritual encouragement, parents and families learn how to nurture relationships and build homes grounded in love and grace. Students are challenged to rise up and become the voice of life on their middle school and high school campuses.

A Refuge in Times of Need

For young women facing unplanned pregnancies, the Hope House is a haven of restoration and renewal. Picture a young woman, estranged from her family, stepping into a place where she is embraced with open arms. The words of Jeremiah 29:11 offer her reassurance: "'For I know the plans I have for you,' declares the Lord, 'plans to prosper you and not to harm you, plans to give you hope and a future.'"

At Hope House Maternity Home, these women are not only given a safe place to stay but are also equipped with skills, resources, and spiritual guidance to navigate a better path for themselves and their children.

A Community Reflecting God's Love

Anchor Point's success is a testament to the faithfulness of God and the generosity of those who believe in its mission. Volunteers and donors, moved by the words of Galatians 6:9, "Let us not become weary in doing good, for at the proper time we will reap a harvest if we do not give up," partner with Anchor Point to bring hope to the hopeless and light to the darkness.

At its helm is Debbie Simmons, a visionary whose leadership and faith have built an organization that embodies the love of Christ. Through her guidance, Anchor Point serves as a reminder of the eternal truth found in **Romans 15:13**, "May the God of hope fill you with all joy and peace as you trust in him, so that you may overflow with hope by the power of the Holy Spirit."

The Anchor of Hope

At Anchor Point, we recognize that the challenges people face often go far beyond surface-level issues. Families come to us burdened by heartbreak, uncertainty, and fear. We know that while practical tools, education, and support are critical, they alone are not enough to bring lasting change. True transformation comes from the saving grace and redeeming power of Jesus. It is a privilege to walk alongside the families we serve and earn the right to share the good news of the One who is the ultimate source of hope.

Through every program and service, we seek to reflect the love of Christ in tangible ways. Whether through counseling, health care, parenting education, or housing, we aim to be the hands and feet of Jesus, showing His compassion, grace, and unconditional love. As relationships of trust are built, we are blessed with opportunities to speak openly about the Savior we love.

For a young woman at Hope House who feels lost and alone, we point to Jesus as the One who promises never to leave or forsake her (Deuteronomy 31:6). For a parent at a Hope Community Initiative who feels unequipped, we remind them that God gives wisdom generously to those who ask (James 1:5). For a woman seeking care at the Obria Medical Clinic, we reflect the truth that she is fearfully and wonderfully made by a Creator who knows her by name (Psalm 139:14).

We don't take these moments lightly. Sharing Jesus is not just a duty; it's our greatest joy and privilege. Every smile we offer, every prayer we pray, and every life we touch is an opportunity to point others to the hope we have found in Him. We are humbled to be part of the story God is writing in the lives of those we serve, and we rejoice in the promise that His Word never returns void (Isaiah 55:11).

In a world that is often unsteady and unpredictable, Anchor Point exists to remind families that there is a firm foundation they can stand on. This foundation is Jesus—our rock, refuge, and anchor. It is in Him that we find not only hope but also peace, joy, and the assurance that we are deeply loved. As we serve our community and beyond, we remain steadfast in our mission to share this hope, knowing it is the greatest gift we can offer.

"We have this hope as an anchor for the soul, firm and secure." This is the promise we cling to, the truth we proclaim, and the joy we share with every family who walks through our doors.

Creating Legacy Both Now and For Eternity

At Anchor Point, we are passionately committed to creating a legacy that extends far beyond the here and now—a legacy that touches lives today and echoes into eternity. Every life we touch, every family we strengthen, and every story of restoration contributes to a ripple effect of hope, faith, and love that reaches outward into the community and forward into the future. Most importantly, we embrace the eternal perspective of our work, knowing that the hope of Jesus we share with those we serve is a treasure that will last forever. This legacy is not just about creating stronger families; it's about pointing hearts toward the One who redeems, restores, and promises an inheritance that will never fade. Through every act of service, we strive to leave a mark that glorifies God and builds a legacy of faith that endures both now and into eternity.

*Anchor Point
Stories of Hope*

Madison's Redemption
Finding Hope and Support in the Face of Fear

Madison, a young woman, found herself in a place she never expected: alone, overwhelmed, and staring at a positive pregnancy test. The test revealed a reality she wasn't ready for and didn't believe she could face. Fear gripped her heart as her world seemed to spiral out of control. Pregnant? It couldn't be. What would she do? Where would she turn? The knot in her stomach tightened as the weight of her situation bore down on her.

Desperate and in need of support, Madison reached for her phone, searching for help. That search led her to Obria Medical Clinic and, eventually, Anchor Point. With a mix of anxiety and cautious hope, she walked through their doors, still unsure of what to expect. What she found was nothing short of life-changing.

The staff at Obria greeted Madison with kindness and warmth, instantly creating a sense of safety in her otherwise chaotic world. One by one, her fears began to surface as she poured out her heart to a caring advocate who listened with genuine compassion. Instead of judgment, Madison received encouragement and reassurance. For the first time, someone told her she could do this—and that she wouldn't have to do it alone.

Then came the ultrasound, a moment Madison would never forget. As the nurse gently guided her through the procedure, the image of her baby appeared on the screen. The tiny heartbeat flickered, and the realization hit her: this was real. A life was growing inside of her. But just as hope began to grow, the nurse hesitated, scanning the image again. Madison's heart raced as she tried to make sense of what was happening. "There's a second baby," the nurse said softly.

Twins. Madison was carrying twins. A tidal wave of emotions washed over her—fear, disbelief, and a fresh wave of anxiety. How could she possibly handle this? She was already struggling to imagine life with one baby, let alone two. Tears threatened to fall as she felt herself slipping back into the despair she had just begun to climb out of.

But once again, the staff at Obria and Anchor Point surrounded her with love and encouragement. They celebrated the news of her twins with her, even as she struggled to process it herself. They reminded her that she wasn't alone and that they would walk alongside her every step of the way. Their reassurance and steadfast support began to chip away at her fear, replacing it with a glimmer of hope.

After the ultrasound, Madison was introduced to The Hope Family Center, a part of Anchor Point's mission to support individuals like her. There, she found another team of caring advocates ready to help. They offered her practical resources, including assistance with Medicaid paperwork, and signed her up for life-on-life sessions with an advocate who would meet with her weekly. Slowly but surely, Madison began to see a path forward.

Having recently moved to Texas from California, Madison had no family or support system nearby, aside from her boyfriend. Anchor Point became the family she didn't have, wrapping her in love, guidance, and the tangible support she needed to face her new reality.

For Madison, the impossible began to feel possible. What started as a story of fear and despair transformed into one of hope and resilience.

Madison's story is only one of many. It's a story of a young woman who, through the love and care of a compassionate community, found the strength to choose life for her children. But there are so many others like Madison—women, men, and families facing unexpected pregnancies, grappling with fear, and searching for hope.

Anchor Point's work—its rescue mission—is only possible because of the generosity and prayers of people who choose to stand with them. Together, hope can be offered to countless others like Madison, reminding them that they are not alone, that they are loved, and that they, too, can find beauty in their journey. Madison's story, once marked by fear, is now a testament to the power of love and community—and it is just one chapter in the greater story of Anchor Point's mission.

Renewed Hope
Manuel and Grace's Journey to Healing and Family Restoration

Manuel and Grace Hernandez's adoption story is a deeply moving testament to resilience, hope, and the transformative power of love. As parents of three children, life became overwhelming during the COVID pandemic, with stress piling on from every direction. Their oldest child was new to their home, emotions were raw, and they were navigating the complexities of adoption amidst a chaotic living situation at their in-laws' house while renovating their own. Each day brought emotional outbursts, tears, and feelings of helplessness.

Desperate for change and a sense of stability, they discovered Hope Camp—a turning point that brought light into their family's struggles. For the children, the camp was a mix of fun and challenge. For Manuel and Grace, it was therapeutic, offering tools and a safe space to process the chaos they were enduring. Initially skeptical about how their children would respond, they were amazed to see their kids engaging and even hurrying to participate, eager to grow.

One of the most profound moments for Manuel was hearing his daughter bravely express feelings she had bottled up: *"I feel alone. I feel like my parents pay more attention to my siblings than to me."* For a father longing to understand his children's hearts, this was a revelation. Witnessing his daughter find her voice and articulate her emotions became a treasured moment—an opportunity for connection and healing.

Grace reflected on how the camp's name, *Hope Camp*, perfectly encapsulated what their family needed. Before attending, their home felt like a battleground, with daily explosions of emotion. But the camp showed them that every tantrum and challenge wasn't just chaos—it was an opportunity. An opportunity to grow, to deepen understanding, and to learn. They began to see that even in their mistakes as parents, there was grace, and hope for healing.

The experience also revealed the strength of the community supporting them. Manuel and Grace were touched by the generosity of donors and staff who made the camp possible. Every meal, every activity, and every moment of respite felt like a tangible expression of love and care. They were overwhelmed by the realization that others had given selflessly so their family could rest, recharge, and heal.

One particularly profound shift came as they embraced their calling in the fostering and adoption journey. Manuel reflected on the immense responsibility of changing the trajectory of a child's life. When he doubted whether their efforts were enough, he was reminded: *"We could be changing the trajectory of hers."* This realization became a cornerstone of their journey, reaffirming their faith and commitment.

Through Hope Camp, the Hernandez's found more than tools and support—they found peace, connection, and a renewed sense of purpose. Their chaotic household became a place of growth, and their struggles turned into stepping stones toward healing. As Grace said, *"Camp was awesome, and I didn't want it to be over."*

This story is one of love in action—of a family choosing to walk the hard path of fostering and adoption, supported by a community that believes in the power of hope. It's a reminder that even in the hardest seasons, transformation is possible, and love can truly change the course of a life.

A Journey of Courage
Naomi's Story of Choosing Life and Finding Love

Naomie's story is a raw and deeply emotional journey of unexpected challenges, overwhelming love, and profound gratitude. She begins with a bright future ahead, coming from a close-knit family and starting college at Texas A&M University of Commerce. She was meeting new people, making connections, and even believed she'd found her "one and only." But life took an unexpected turn when a relationship ended, and the very next day, Naomi discovered she was pregnant.

The news hit like a storm. What should have been a moment of support and reassurance became a lonely and confusing night, filled with talk of abortion costs instead of comfort. Fear and uncertainty gripped her. Naomi didn't know what to do, but deep down, she felt a glimmer of determination—an instinct to fight for the life she now carried, even when she doubted her ability to do so.

Her mom stepped in, scheduling an appointment at Obria, where Naomi saw her baby's heartbeat for the first time. That moment changed everything. The sound of that tiny heartbeat ignited something in her—a fierce, unshakable resolve. She didn't fully understand the joy she felt, but she knew she would do whatever it took to give her child the best life possible.

Determined to prepare for her new reality, Naomiined parenting classes at Anchor Point. She feared judgment but instead found a community that embraced her without hesitation. She could be herself, open and vulnerable, and for the first time, she realized she wasn't alone in this journey.

The months flew by, and before she knew it, the moment she both anticipated and feared arrived. Her baby was born, and when they placed him in her arms, all she could think was, *"Perfect. He's so beautiful."* In that instant, her life transformed.

The love she felt was overwhelming—like a physical weight on her chest, so powerful she couldn't contain it. She had never imagined she could love someone this deeply, and it was love that gave her the strength to carry on, no matter how hard it might get.

Looking back, Naomi wishes she could go back and comfort the younger version of herself—the girl sobbing on the bathroom floor, paralyzed by fear. She wishes she could tell her that this beautiful ending was waiting, that the love she would feel for her son would be worth every challenge.

Now, as a mother, Naomi feels an ache when she's away from her son, a love so strong it feels almost unbearable. She's also deeply grateful. The support from Anchor Point didn't just help her—it completely changed her life. It wasn't just a charitable gesture or a kind act; it was a lifeline, a gift that saved her and gave her son the chance to thrive.

Through tears, she says, *"Thank you. You didn't just help me. You gave my son his life, and you changed mine forever."* Naomi's story is one of fear transformed into hope, and hope into love—a love that now defines her world.

From Chaos to Connection
Waylon and Lily's Journey of Family Transformation

Waylon and Lily Miller's story is a heartfelt journey of love, challenges, and transformation within their family of seven. As parents of five children, including adopted kids, they faced unique struggles—gaps in education, challenging behaviors, and the difficulty of understanding the hidden hurts their children carried. The behaviors were often cries for help, rooted in pain, and the Milleres worked tirelessly to bridge the emotional and educational gaps.

Then came camp, a pivotal experience for their family. The camp's thoughtful design paired each child with a buddy whose presence seemed divinely orchestrated. These buddies weren't just caretakers—they became safe, nurturing mentors who guided, challenged, and invested in the kids' lives. For Waylon and Lily, stepping back and allowing others to lead their children was an act of trust that paid off in ways they couldn't have imagined. Their children thrived under the mentorship of these compassionate guides, learning about boundaries, safe people, and trust.

One of the most powerful moments for Lily came during her one-on-one time with Miss Debbie, who saw and validated her pain for the first time. "What happened wasn't okay," Debbie told her, and that acknowledgment alone began to mend wounds that had been buried for years. Lily felt the healing touch of someone who truly understood her struggles, believing that God was using this moment to bring restoration to the deepest parts of her heart.

For Waylon, a defining moment occurred when his son shared a heartbreaking story from before their adoption. Waylon, already emotionally connected after bonding with his daughter earlier, found himself overwhelmed by the weight of his son's words. Sitting with his child, he let his tears flow, showing raw, unfiltered emotion. For his son, seeing his dad process this pain in such a vulnerable way was a profound moment of connection and understanding. It was a healing experience for both father and son, bridging a gap that words alone couldn't mend.

Camp wasn't just a temporary escape—it was a transformative experience for the entire family. Unlike traditional counseling, which sometimes felt isolating, this was something they all went through together. All seven family members shared the same experiences, learned the same language, and gained the same tools. This unity became the foundation for a new chapter in their family's journey.

Waylon and Lily walked away from camp with a renewed sense of hope. They no longer felt like they were fumbling through parenting challenges alone while dragging their kids behind them. Instead, they felt empowered as a team, equipped to move forward with shared understanding and purpose. Camp taught them that healing and growth happen best when everyone is on the same page, working together as a family.

Reflecting on the experience, Waylon and Lily know it was absolutely worth the investment. Camp didn't just change the way they parent—it reshaped their family's story. Now, they move forward with hope, unity, and the belief that even the deepest hurts can lead to profound healing when approached with love, patience, and faith.

Gina's Redemption
From Brokenness to a Life Renewed by Hope"

When Gina walked into Obria Medical Clinic earlier this year, her face carried the weight of a past filled with pain, regret, and brokenness. Her story was one of heartbreak—a story not unlike so many others who seek help. Gina had endured a lifetime of struggles: four abortions, a history of abuse, a battle with drug addiction, and the constant voice in her head telling her she was a failure. She was the mother of an 8-year-old but carried the heavy burden of believing she wasn't good enough for him, let alone the precious new life growing inside her.

But there was a flicker of light in Gina's story. She was 5 months sober—a milestone that marked her commitment to a better future. However, she felt lost, uncertain how to move forward or how to become the mother her unborn child deserved. Her past haunted her, whispering lies that she couldn't escape her mistakes, that she would never be enough. Despite her fears, she walked through the doors of Obria, hoping for something more.

Our nurses immediately embraced Gina with compassion and understanding, recognizing not only her pain but also her courage. They celebrated her sobriety—a monumental achievement—and rejoiced with her over the new life she was carrying. Together, they acknowledged her incredible strength to fight through her struggles and take the first step toward healing. Gina needed more than medical care; she needed hope, healing, and the assurance that she was not defined by her past.

During her appointment, Gina saw her baby on the ultrasound screen for the first time. The tiny, miraculous life growing inside her sparked a new determination in her heart.

Tears streamed down her face as she watched the screen, overwhelmed by the reality that this baby wasn't a mistake but a chance for redemption—a fresh start. Our nurses reassured her that she was not alone and connected her with our Hope Family Center to ensure she had the support she needed every step of the way.

At the Hope Family Center, Gina found a safe place where she could learn to prepare for motherhood and work through her pain. She enrolled in parenting and prenatal classes, and we helped her gather material resources for her baby, ensuring she had everything she needed to welcome her child into the world. But the journey didn't end there. Gina's heart carried deep wounds from her past abortions, wounds that needed healing. She was introduced to our Abortion Recovery class, a program designed to help women release the guilt, shame, and sorrow they carry and embrace the transformative power of forgiveness and grace.

For Gina, the Abortion Recovery class was a turning point. Through this program, she began to confront the pain she had buried for so long and found the courage to let go of the lies that told her she wasn't enough. Slowly but surely, her heart began to heal, and she started to see herself as the strong, capable, and loving mother she was meant to be.

Gina's journey is far from over, but she is no longer walking it alone. With every class, every connection, and every ounce of love and support from the Obria and Hope Family Center teams, she is breaking free from the chains of her past. She is building a new future for herself and her children—a future filled with hope, healing, and the promise of generational change.

Gina's story reminds us of the power of compassion, the importance of a loving community, and the incredible strength of a mother's love. Your support makes stories like Gina's possible, providing not only the material resources but also the emotional and spiritual care that transforms lives. Because of you, Gina is no longer defined by her past but by her courage and the hope she has found for the future.

Thank you for standing with us as we celebrate Gina's redemption and the new life she is bringing into the world. Together, we are helping to heal broken hearts and bring hope to those who need it most.

Healing Together
Finding Freedom Through the Recovery Journey

Picture this: you're standing in a grocery store checkout line, surrounded by women going about their day. Or sitting in the stands at a high school football game, watching cheerleaders perform, the marching band play, and the color guard twirl in synchronized harmony. Maybe you're at work, in a meeting with female coworkers, or enjoying coffee with a group of friends or family members.

Now consider this staggering reality: one in four women you see—friends, neighbors, colleagues—has reported being sexually abused. One in four will experience an abortion in her lifetime. These aren't faceless statistics. They represent real women—women in your life, women in your community. They carry deep wounds, often in silence, hidden beneath layers of shame, fear, and isolation.

At Anchor Point, we refuse to ignore this pain. We walk boldly into the hard places, determined to be a source of hope and healing. We believe in a God who restores, who takes what is broken and makes it whole, who transforms even the most painful past into a story of redemption.

Imagine a woman who has carried the weight of sexual abuse for years, feeling unseen and unheard, her pain locked away. She walks into Anchor Point for the first time, unsure of what to expect. There, she finds a safe space—compassionate listeners who don't shy away from her story, a community that assures her she's not alone. Slowly, her walls begin to crumble, and the healing begins. She starts to believe that she is not defined by what happened to her, that her worth is unshakable, and that her life can be filled with hope.

Think of another woman, perhaps a young mother, who has silently carried the weight of a past abortion. She's haunted by feelings of guilt and shame, convinced she can't be forgiven. But through Anchor Point, she discovers grace—a love that meets her where she is and offers freedom from the chains of her past. She learns that her story doesn't end in regret but in redemption, and she walks away renewed, her heart lighter than it's been in years.

This is what happens at Anchor Point every day. It's a place where healing is more than a possibility—it's a reality. It's where pain is met with compassion, and lives are transformed by the truth of God's promises. Isaiah 40:4 tells us that God makes the crooked places straight and the rough places smooth. This is the foundation of everything we do—helping women see that even in their deepest pain, God has a plan, a plan to heal, restore, and bring beauty from ashes.

Take a moment to think about the courage it takes to confront these wounds. These women are not just statistics—they are warriors, brave enough to step into the light and seek healing. And they are not alone. They are surrounded by supporters, people like you who care deeply and give generously to make this work possible.

As you reflect on this, we ask for your prayers. Pray for the women we serve, that they may find hope and freedom. Pray for our leaders, who pour their hearts into walking alongside these women. And pray about how God might be calling you to join us in this mission, whether through prayer, support, or sharing this message of hope with others.

Galatians 5:1 declares, *"It is for freedom that Christ came to set us free."* That freedom is not just a promise; it's happening here and now. Thank you for being a part of this work. Together, we are not only changing lives—we are rewriting stories, bringing hope where there was none, and reminding every woman we serve that she is deeply loved and valued. May you, too, be blessed as you walk alongside us in this life-changing mission.

From Overwhelmed to Empowered
Abigail's Story of Healing and Hope

Abigail, a young mother of a 13-month-old baby boy named Luke, opens up about her journey of transformation, love, and healing as she navigates the challenges of raising a blended family. Her world shifted when her stepdaughter, Destiny, moved in just weeks before David was born. The timing was overwhelming, as her family was already under stress from a year and a half of court proceedings. While Abigail and her husband wanted to give Destiny a stable, loving home, they struggled to bridge the emotional gaps and address the behaviors Destiny displayed.

Through the court's recommendation, they sought a counselor who could provide guidance not only for Destiny but for the entire family. That search led them to Anchor Point, where they found a counselor who became a lifeline. With her wisdom and kindness, she helped the family begin the healing process. For the first time, Destiny had a safe space to express her feelings, and Abigail and her husband learned how to truly hear her, understanding the unspoken hurts behind her actions.

Destiny's transformation was incredible. With her counselor's help, she developed practical tools to manage her emotions, like journaling. Abigail recalls buying Destiny a beautiful journal, complete with colorful pens and markers, and watching as Destiny poured her heart into it. A new reward system and the concept of a "redo" helped Destiny replace negative behaviors with positive actions. If she said something unkind or acted out, she could try again in a safe and encouraging environment, earning praise for her efforts. This approach brought light into Destiny's life, and Abigail saw her stepdaughter begin to thrive in ways she hadn't before.

The counselor didn't just focus on Destiny—she extended her support to Abigail and her husband, teaching them how to parent in a blended family. For Abigail, this was no small feat. She had to learn how to balance the emotional strain of court issues with the tenderness required to be both a mother and a stepmother. It was difficult, but the counselor's wisdom gave them the tools to navigate the complexities of their family dynamic. Abigail says this guidance was nothing short of life-changing, helping her become the mother Destiny needed her to be.

Abigail's gratitude for Anchor Point overflows. Beyond counseling, the organization provided her with essential resources during some of her hardest moments. Diapers, clothes, toiletries—everything her baby needed—were lovingly provided, along with spiritual guidance, Bible studies, and parenting classes. Abigail felt seen, supported, and cared for in ways that lifted her during times of uncertainty. She credits Anchor Point with not only helping her family heal but also helping her grow into a stronger, more confident mother.

Her heart is now filled with a mission to give back. Abigail shares her story with other mothers and pregnant women, offering them the hope and encouragement she received. She passes out business cards and tells anyone who will listen about the life-changing work of Anchor Point. For her, this is more than a personal mission—it's a calling from God. She believes He has placed this desire in her heart, and she is determined to follow His plan, spreading hope and love to others in their time of need.

Through tears of gratitude, Abigail reflects on her journey. She knows her family's story is one of redemption and grace—a testament to the power of love, support, and faith. She prays that others will experience the same transformation she has, finding hope and healing even in life's most challenging moments.

Finding Hope
Sandra's Journey to Becoming the Mother Her Children Deserve

Sandra's story is one of resilience, transformation, and the power of love in parenting. As a mother of four, she faced a life that felt like constant chaos—hectic, overwhelming, and full of moments where she felt helpless. When tough situations arose, she didn't know how to respond and often found herself reacting with frustration or anger. She longed for a better way but wasn't sure where to start. When she heard about the Pathway to Hope Camp, she decided to take a chance, desperate for tools and answers to become the mother her children needed. What she found at camp changed everything.

Before camp, Sandra struggled with feelings of inadequacy. Parenting felt like an uphill battle, with no clear path forward. But camp offered her not just guidance, but also hope. It helped her see her family—and herself—through a new lens. She learned to shift her focus from the small mistakes her children made to the many wonderful things they were doing right. Instead of fixating on the 10 percent that wasn't perfect, she began celebrating the 90 percent they were getting right. This simple yet profound shift opened her eyes to the beauty and strengths of her children, helping her become a more positive and present mother.

One tool that stood out to Sandra was the puzzle jar—a tangible way to affirm her children's positive traits. By focusing on their strengths and celebrating their beautiful characteristics, she discovered how impactful compliments and encouragement could be. She also learned the importance of nurturing her children emotionally, even in seemingly small moments. For example, offering a band-aid when her kids got hurt, even if there wasn't a visible mark, became a way to show them that she cared deeply about their feelings. To her children, that small act meant the world. It built trust and reminded them that their mom would always be there for them.

At camp, Sandra also discovered the power of effective communication. She learned to replace long, drawn-out lectures—which often left her children tuned out—with short, impactful phrases like "with respect," "compromise," and "cooperate." These simple words became powerful tools that grabbed her children's attention, resolved conflicts quickly, and created a more peaceful home environment. With these tools, she began approaching parenting challenges with calm and clarity, rather than frustration and confusion.

But the transformation wasn't just about parenting techniques. It was deeply personal for Sandra. Camp helped her realize that she wasn't a "bad mom," as she had sometimes feared. She was simply a mom who needed a little help, and now she had the tools to succeed. With the skills and insights she gained, she discovered that it's never too late to make changes and repair relationships. Her children's unconditional love reminded her that mistakes could be forgiven, and with intentional effort, she could build a stronger bond with them.

Leaving camp, Sandra felt like a new person. She not only had hope but a renewed sense of confidence in her ability to guide her children with love and patience. She saw her family as a team and parenting as a journey she didn't have to navigate alone. The tools she gained became a foundation for growth, not just for her children but for her as well.

Now, Sandra shares her story to encourage other parents. She wants them to know that no matter how hard things may seem, it's never too late to change. "Your kids love you," she says. "They will forgive you, and with the right tools, you can build something beautiful together."

Pathway to Hope Camp didn't just give Sandra parenting skills—it gave her the freedom to embrace who she is as a mother, flaws and all. It gave her the courage to move forward with love, hope, and purpose. Her story is a powerful reminder that no matter where you start, transformation is possible, and the love of a parent can overcome any challenge when guided by hope and faith.

Breaking Free
Gianna's Journey of Healing Through Anchor Point's Abortion Recovery Group

Gianna's story is one of deep pain, healing, and redemption—a journey from shame and secrecy to freedom and purpose. For years, she carried the weight of having had three abortions, a burden she kept hidden from others and avoided confronting herself. As she walked with God over the past two years, she felt Him calling her to face this painful part of her past, to work through the hurt she had buried, and to find healing. This was not an easy step; it was one filled with fear and uncertainty.

Through Anchor Point's Abortion Recovery Group, Gianna found a safe space to begin her journey. At first, she was terrified and hesitant. The thought of opening up about her past was overwhelming, and she wasn't sure what to expect. But as the process unfolded, something incredible happened—it became freeing. Slowly, the chains of guilt and shame that had held her for so long began to break. What once felt like an impossible weight to bear was lifted, and she began to experience God's grace and forgiveness in a powerful way.

The journey was not without its challenges. Gianna described how difficult it was to work through her emotions, knowing that healing required confronting her pain head-on. She felt the resistance of fear and shame, a battle she recognized as the enemy trying to keep her from breaking free. But she also felt God's unwavering love, His assurance that He had already forgiven her, and His desire for her to walk in freedom.

Gianna now looks back on her experience with Anchor Point's Abortion Recovery Group as one of the most liberating and transformative parts of her life. The program not only helped her heal but also helped her rediscover herself.

She realized how many women, just like her, carry the silent pain of abortion, hiding it from the world and from themselves. She feels compelled to tell these women that freedom is possible—that God loves them and wants to redeem their stories, just as He did for her.

Her gratitude to Anchor Point's Abortion Recovery Group is immense. It became the light she had been searching for, showing her the way out of darkness. With a renewed sense of purpose, Gianna is determined to give back. She shares her testimony courageously, showing others that healing is possible. She collects baby clothes for Anchor Point, wanting to help other mothers who need support, and she speaks about her experience in her church community, hoping to reach those who are still searching for hope.

Gianna's story is a powerful reminder of God's love and forgiveness. She says, "I wish I could tell the whole world what it's like to go through post-abortion recovery. It's so liberating, so life-changing." Her journey is a testament to the transformative power of grace, the strength of vulnerability, and the importance of a community like Anchor Point that walks alongside women in their most challenging moments. In her words, "Anchor Point is changing the world, one life at a time."

Breaking Barriers
The Phillips Family's Journey to Healing and Connection

The Phillips family's story is one of transformation, connection, and breaking free from the cycle of frustration and disconnection, particularly with their teenage son, who came to them after experiencing significant pain and trauma. As parents of an adopted child, they faced unique challenges that often accompany a young boy navigating the complexities of trust, identity, and healing from past hurts.

Their son's defiance and rebellion often felt like a wall they couldn't break through. Simple requests, like completing chores or following rules, would turn into explosive battles. He resisted authority, refusing to do what he was asked, and his behaviors often felt intentionally provocative. Beneath the surface, though, they began to realize that his actions were rooted in something much deeper—feelings of abandonment, mistrust, and fear. These emotions, born from his painful past, were manifesting as anger and defiance.

The emotional scars from his earlier experiences often left him unable to articulate what he was feeling. Instead of expressing sadness or fear, he would lash out or shut down completely. At times, he would test their love and patience, almost as if he was expecting them to give up on him, just as others might have in the past. His behaviors pushed every button they had, leading to constant conflict and feelings of helplessness.

Adding to the difficulty, their son struggled with regulating his emotions. A small disappointment could trigger an outburst, and the tools they were using—yelling, grounding, or physical activities like push-ups—only seemed to escalate the situation. He also had difficulty connecting with others, often retreating into himself or lashing out at peers, which left him feeling isolated. As parents, they felt like they were on a roller coaster, trying the same ineffective strategies over and over again, and they couldn't see a way forward.

At camp, the family learned to approach these challenges differently. Instead of reacting to his defiance, they began focusing on his heart—what was he really trying to say? For example, when he refused to follow a simple instruction, they learned to pause and ask themselves, "What need is he trying to express?" They discovered that his rebellion often stemmed from a fear of failure or rejection, feelings that had been deeply ingrained from his early experiences. By responding with compassion instead of frustration, they started to rebuild trust.

One of the most transformative lessons was understanding the importance of emotional validation. They learned that even small gestures, like listening without judgment or offering a hug after an outburst, could create a safe space for their son to express his emotions. For instance, when he became angry over a seemingly minor issue, they stopped focusing on correcting the behavior and instead focused on the underlying emotion—hurt or fear. This shift helped him feel seen and heard, which was crucial for a boy who had spent much of his life feeling invisible.

Another breakthrough came from learning a consistent, calming approach to communication. Their son had previously struggled with the mixed messages he received from their differing parenting styles. But at camp, they unified their language, using the same short, clear phrases to communicate expectations and boundaries. For example, instead of long lectures that overwhelmed him, they used phrases like, "Let's work together," or, "We respect each other here." This consistency gave their son a sense of security, knowing that both parents were on the same page.

Over the course of camp, they began to see the walls around their son's heart come down. At first, it was subtle—fleeting moments of eye contact, a quiet response to a question. But day by day, these moments grew. One evening, their son surprised them by opening up about a painful memory from his past. It was raw and heartbreaking, but it was also a breakthrough—a moment of trust that they had been longing for. For a boy who had learned to protect himself by shutting others out, this was a profound step toward healing.

The Phillips family's story is a testament to the resilience of love and the power of compassion. They faced the unique challenges of parenting a teenage boy who carried the weight of a painful past, but with patience, understanding, and the tools they gained at camp, they began to break the cycle of frustration and disconnection. Now, they are united as a family, speaking the same language of love, trust, and hope. It's a story of transformation—one where a child's pain is met with unwavering support, and a family learns that healing is possible, even in the face of the hardest struggles.

Stella's Leap of Faith
Building a Future of Hope for Her Baby Boy

Stella's story is one of resilience and determination in the face of incredible challenges. When she discovered she was pregnant with her first baby, a precious boy due in early October, her life was anything but stable. Living in California with most of her family, Stella made the courageous decision to move to Texas to be near her brother, hoping to build a better life. But life quickly took a difficult turn. Stella and her brother found themselves homeless, and her boyfriend, having lost his job, couldn't renew his lease.

Newly pregnant and without a roof over her head, Stella was consumed by fear and uncertainty. She was desperate to find a safe place to prepare for her baby's arrival, but the journey was riddled with heartbreak. She reached out to several support organizations in Houston, but with the city's large population in need and the added complications of COVID protocols, she was repeatedly turned away. Each rejection deepened her panic and sense of helplessness. Yet, even in the darkness, Stella refused to give up hope.

Her persistence led her to discover **Hope House Maternity Home**, and that discovery changed everything. From the moment Stella walked through the doors, she felt a sense of stability she hadn't known in months. For the first time in a long time, she could breathe. At Hope House, she found not only a place to call home but also a supportive community and the resources she needed to plan for her future.

With a safe environment and a team that believed in her, Stella began to dream again. Her fears turned into determination, and she set her sights on building a stable, beautiful life for her baby boy. Hope House offered her opportunities she never thought possible. With their help, Stella mapped out a plan to prepare for her son's arrival while also laying the foundation for her education and career.

Stella is taking a monumental leap forward. After giving birth to her son, she will begin her journey back to college. Her first step is completing a few math courses to prepare for a nursing program—a dream she is finally able to pursue. Stella is driven to create a life of stability and opportunity for her little family, and her unwavering resolve inspires everyone around her.

Stella's success wouldn't have been possible without the love and support she found at Hope House and the generosity of the Anchor Point community. Your contributions—whether through prayers, time, or donations—have given Stella the stability and resources she needed to overcome homelessness and prepare for motherhood with confidence. Thanks to you, Stella has a safe place to call home, the support to nurture her dreams, and the tools to build a brighter future for herself and her baby boy. Her journey is a testament to the power of hope, love, and perseverance, and she is well on her way to achieving the life she's always dreamed of.

Thank you for being a part of Stella's story, for believing in her, and for helping her take this incredible leap of faith. Together, we are not just meeting immediate needs but also planting seeds for a future filled with hope, love, and endless possibilities.

Anchored in Hope
Lisa's Journey of Serving and Seeing Lives Transformed

Lisa's story as a volunteer with Anchor Point is a heartfelt testament to the profound joy and growth that come from serving others. For her, volunteering isn't just about giving—it's about receiving so much more in return. *"I've grown spiritually so much here,"* she shares, her voice full of emotion. *"Seeing God work, seeing someone come in so broken and then watching their transformation—it's incredible."*

Lisa recalls one of the many moments that left an indelible mark on her heart. She speaks of Caitlin and Anthony, a couple who came to Anchor Point early in her volunteering journey. They were scared, uncertain, and considering abortion. They hadn't been dating long and were looking for hope in a time of overwhelming doubt. Through compassionate conversations, education, and support, they made the brave decision to parent their child. From that moment, everything changed.

The couple became deeply involved in Anchor Point's programs, embracing not just parenting education but spiritual growth. Both Caitlin and Anthony found faith, giving their lives to Christ. Lisa beams with pride as she describes how their baby is now being raised in a Christian home, surrounded by love and hope. *"Their lives have been transformed,"* she says, *"not just for now, but for eternity. The difference is incredible."*

Her joy doesn't stop there. Lisa also finds deep fulfillment in financially supporting Anchor Point. *"This center does so much for our community, and it has the potential to do even more,"* she explains. She believes in the mission wholeheartedly, knowing that her contributions are part of something much greater—God's kingdom work.

When asked why others should get involved, Lisa's answer is filled with passion: *"The time you spend here will bless the rest of your life more than you can imagine."* She reflects on how humbling it is to be used by God in such a meaningful way. *"To think that God could take me and use me to transform lives—it's overwhelming. You're literally on the front lines, making a difference for eternity."*

For Lisa, volunteering at Anchor Point isn't just an act of service; it's a life-changing journey. It's a place where brokenness meets healing, where hope is born, and where she has experienced firsthand the beauty of being part of something so much bigger than herself. Through tears of gratitude, she encourages others to step in, to give, and to serve: *"You'll be blessed more than you can imagine. You'll witness miracles, and you'll feel God's hand in every moment."*

Anchor Point is more than just an organization—it's a source of light in dark places. It offers a lifeline to those who feel hopeless, providing not just practical resources but a community of love, faith, and compassion. Whether it's a struggling couple finding redemption, a young mother finding confidence, or a volunteer like Lisa finding purpose, Anchor Point is a beacon of hope, showing that transformation is possible, healing is real, and lives can be changed forever.

Ali's Journey
Rising from the Ashes to Build a Life of Love and Hope

Ali's story is one of resilience, hope, and the transformative power of love. Her life before arriving at Hope House was marked by immense challenges and heartache. She had endured traumatic experiences that left her questioning her own worth and ability to move forward. For a time, she lived in a shelter for women who had survived domestic abuse—a refuge but not the stable foundation she needed for her future.

When Ali discovered she was pregnant, a tidal wave of emotions washed over her. She was overwhelmed by fear, uncertainty, and doubt. Could she really parent her child? Could she break free from her painful past to create a safe, loving environment for her baby? The trauma she had endured made her doubt her ability to be the mother her child deserved. Adoption seemed like a viable option—an act of love to give her baby a better life than she thought she could provide. Yet, deep within her heart, Ali longed to be the one to love, nurture, and raise her baby. Despite her fears, her love for her unborn child grew stronger with each passing day.

Ali knew that if she wanted to parent her baby, she needed to start fresh—to find a safe haven where she could heal, grow, and prepare for the incredible responsibility of motherhood. She reached out to Hope House, a decision that would mark the beginning of her transformation.

From the moment Ali walked through the doors of Hope House, her journey began to change. She found more than just a roof over her head; she found a community that believed in her and supported her. The Anchor Point Network provided her with access to vital resources, counseling, and the tools she needed to build a brighter future. For the first time in a long time, Ali felt safe, seen, and empowered.

Ali's determination to be the best mom she could be became her driving force. She set her sights on learning new skills and pursuing an education that would allow her to build a stable, fulfilling career in the medical field. Week by week, she made strides, balancing her preparations for motherhood with the hard work of healing from her past. Through it all, her love for her baby gave her the strength to keep moving forward.

Mother's Day was a milestone for Ali and the other moms at Hope House—a day filled with hope and celebration. For Ali, it was a reminder of how far she had come and how much she had overcome to embrace her new role as a mother. Surrounded by love and encouragement from the Anchor Point community, Ali felt a renewed sense of purpose. Her journey is far from over, but she is already proving to herself and her baby that they deserve a life filled with love, safety, and opportunity.

Ali's story is a testament to the power of hope and the resilience of the human spirit. With every step forward, she is not only rewriting her own story but also laying the foundation for her child's future. She is a shining example of what can happen when a young mom is given the support, resources, and love she needs to rise above her circumstances and create a new beginning.

Thank you to everyone who supports Hope House and the Anchor Point Network. Your prayers, time, and donations make all the difference. Because of you, young moms like Ali have the chance to turn their dreams into reality and to give their children a brighter, more hopeful future.

From Struggles to Strength
The Diaz Family's Journey of Hope and Connection

The Diaz family's story is a powerful testament to perseverance, love, and the hope that transformation is possible, even in the face of overwhelming challenges. As parents of both biological and adopted children, they faced the unique complexities of raising a family with diverse needs. Their youngest child, struggling with developmental delays and intense emotional responses to frustration, was at the heart of many difficulties. His reactions—often disproportionate to the situation—left the entire family feeling strained, disconnected, and unsure of how to move forward.

Life felt like an endless cycle of frustration, and the emotional toll it took was heavy. For the Diazs, the tension extended beyond just their child—it was felt by everyone. Each meltdown seemed to widen the gap, leaving them feeling more like individuals battling chaos than a united family. They wanted so desperately to help their youngest thrive, but they didn't know how. That's when they turned to Pathway to Hope Camp, longing for tools, connection, and a way forward.

What they found at camp wasn't just answers—it was a lifeline. From the moment they arrived, they felt a shift. The camp provided something they hadn't experienced in a long time: moments of joy and togetherness. Whether it was participating in playful relay races or silly activities like shaving parents, the camp created opportunities for laughter—something that had felt distant for so long. These moments of lightness began to dissolve the tension that had taken root in their family.

One of the most profound lessons they learned was how to address their youngest child's behaviors in a way that fostered growth rather than conflict. They discovered the importance of practicing desired behaviors in safe, calm environments. For example, instead of waiting for a meltdown, they would create opportunities to rehearse responses when their child felt secure, guiding him gently toward better reactions. This approach gave their son a sense of control and confidence, which started to carry over into real-life situations.

Watching their son respond positively was a revelation. It was the first glimpse of hope they had felt in a long time—a sign that change was not just possible but already happening. Each small victory, whether it was a calmer response to frustration or a successful "redo" of a challenging behavior, felt monumental. Their son's progress became a spark of healing for the entire family.

But the transformation didn't stop with their youngest child. One of the most beautiful aspects of camp was that it brought everyone together. The children weren't just observers in their parents' learning—they were part of the process. They saw their mom and dad learning, playing, and practicing the same tools alongside them. For the first time in a long time, the Diazs felt like a team. Everyone was learning the same language, creating a consistency and unity that had been missing.

The emotional breakthroughs came in both big and small ways. The laughter of a relay race, the joy of watching their children cheer them on, and the quiet moments of understanding between parent and child all added up to something transformative. As the days passed, the family began to feel the walls come down—not just around their youngest child's heart but around their own hearts, too. They saw glimpses of their children's trust and felt the power of connection being rebuilt, brick by brick.

For the Diazs, the greatest gift from camp was hope. In just a few weeks, they saw progress that had once felt out of reach. Their youngest child, who had been a source of such struggle, became a source of inspiration as he started to blossom. Their biological and adopted children alike began to thrive, each taking meaningful steps forward. The family as a whole felt renewed, united by a shared journey and the tools to keep moving forward. Looking back, the Diazs are overcome with gratitude. They've seen firsthand the impact that intentional learning, compassion, and connection can have on a family. With tears in their eyes, they express a wish that every adoptive family could have the same experience: "I wish this was available for every adoptive family. It should be."

Their story is one of struggle, yes, but also of triumph. It's a story about finding light in the darkness, rebuilding trust, and rediscovering the joy of being a family. Through the laughter, the hard work, and the breakthroughs, they found what they had been searching for all along: hope. And with that hope, they've been given the strength to keep loving, growing, and walking forward together.

A Beacon of Hope: Chloe's Story of Finding Strength and Renewal

Chloe's story is one of fear, transformation, and the incredible power of hope. Two years ago, her world was filled with uncertainty and loneliness. Discovering she was pregnant should have been a joyful moment, but instead, it brought overwhelming fear. She didn't have insurance to cover her pregnancy, didn't know where to go or what to do, and felt completely alone. Terrified and desperate, she reached out for help, not knowing if she'd find it. Someone pointed her to Anchor Point, and she walked through its doors hoping to get a pregnancy test for Medicaid—nothing more. But what she found there was life-changing.

Walking into Anchor Point for the first time, Chloe was nervous and unsure of what to expect. The unfamiliarity of the space only heightened her anxiety. She planned to get in and out as quickly as possible. But then, a small miracle happened—she saw Shelly, someone she had known from high school band. That small connection felt like a lifeline, a flicker of familiarity in a sea of uncertainty. Shelly's warmth and kindness helped ease Chloe's fears, and as they talked, Chloe began to realize that Anchor Point wasn't just a clinic. It was a place filled with people who truly cared, a place where brokenness could turn into something beautiful.

One of the most transformative parts of Chloe's journey was meeting Romina, her spiritual counselor. At the time, Chloe felt completely disconnected from God. She was spiritually empty, broken, and convinced she had been forgotten. She didn't even know where to begin. But Romina didn't just listen—she poured her heart into Chloe's healing. Romina checked on her weekly, offering prayer, encouragement, and an unwavering presence. She asked about the baby, her health, and her fears, making Chloe feel truly seen and cared for. Slowly, session by session, Chloe's faith began to grow. She found a church where she could nurture her spiritual journey, and for the first time in years, she felt God's presence filling the emptiness.

The hope Chloe found extended far beyond spiritual healing. Romina connected her with resources to secure child care and guided her toward finding a job. Those connections became stepping stones that led Chloe to a career with the city of Dayton. What started as a terrifying and uncertain pregnancy turned into an opportunity to build a stable, fulfilling future for herself and her son.

Hope also came in the form of her growing bond with her son. Chloe lights up as she talks about him—his curiosity, his joy, and his sweet personality. She marvels at how this once overwhelming challenge has turned into her greatest blessing. He's smart, funny, and full of life, even as he approaches the "terrible twos" with all the energy and determination of a toddler. For Chloe, he is a daily reminder of how far she's come and how much she has to be grateful for.

Reflecting on her journey, Chloe's heart swells with gratitude for Anchor Point and everyone who helped her along the way. "Thank you to everyone who played a part, big or small," she says, her voice heavy with emotion. "I've seen how Anchor Point has helped not just me but so many others. Whenever I meet someone who needs help, I always send them here because I know they'll be taken care of."

One of the moments that filled Chloe with the most hope was witnessing how Anchor Point transformed not just her life but the lives of others. She saw women come in broken, unsure of their worth or future, and watched as they gained confidence, resources, and the faith to rebuild their lives. There were mothers who arrived terrified and left with the assurance that they were not alone, families who found stability, and women who discovered God's love for the first time. These stories, alongside her own, remind Chloe that Anchor Point is so much more than a program—it's a beacon of hope.

If Chloe had to sum up her experience with Anchor Point in one word, it would be *hope*. Hope when she felt forgotten. Hope when she didn't know where to turn. Hope that gave her strength to face her challenges and see the blessings waiting on the other side. Anchor Point didn't just change her circumstances—it changed her life, showing her that even in the darkest moments, there is always a way forward. And for Chloe, that hope will always shine brightly as a reminder of what's possible when love and faith meet courage and grace.

David's Second Chance
A Journey of Redemption, Hope, and Purpose

David's story is one of redemption, purpose, and the overwhelming desire to bring hope to others. After being given a second chance at life, he felt a powerful calling to make a difference. He created *Run for Health*, an initiative that combined his passion for running with his dream of inspiring healthier choices and stronger communities. But more than that, David hoped his efforts would touch lives so deeply that one day, someone would sit across from him and say, "You made a difference—you gave me hope."

When David began searching for a nonprofit to partner with, he had a clear vision of what he wanted: a small, local organization where every dollar could make an immediate and tangible impact. When he discovered Anchor Point, he knew he had found something special. From his very first visit, he was struck by the warmth and passion of the team. As he walked through the doors, he was greeted with smiles and a genuine sense of purpose. The people at Anchor Point weren't just doing a job—they were living their mission, pouring love and care into every person they served.

During his tour, David shared the story behind *Run for Health*. As he spoke with the team, he realized how deeply their goals aligned. He had created his initiative to inspire hope and change, and Anchor Point existed to do the very same thing—transforming lives and bringing healing to those in need. It was a perfect partnership, and David left that day knowing he had found a cause worth supporting.

Over the years, *Run for Health* has become a powerful tool for good. Despite setbacks like weather challenges that affected event participation, David's initiative has raised tens of thousands of dollars to support Anchor Point's work. But for

David, it's not just about the financial contributions. It's about being part of something greater—seeing lives transformed, hope restored, and families brought back from the brink.

One of the most profound moments in David's journey came through his personal spiritual awakening. After years of searching, he found a sense of belonging and purpose he had never known before. His baptism marked a turning point in his life. Standing in the water that day, surrounded by people who loved and supported him, he felt an overwhelming peace and joy. For the first time, he had a church home and a church family, and the feeling of being truly seen and accepted was life-changing.

Reflecting on his journey, David speaks with deep emotion about the impact of Anchor Point. He shares how much he has learned from the team, particularly Debbie and Scott Simmons, whose passion and dedication have inspired him in ways they may never fully realize. "They'll never know how much I've learned from them," he says, his voice filled with gratitude. Through their example, he has discovered what it means to serve selflessly, to give generously, and to bring hope to those who need it most.

For David, Anchor Point is more than just a nonprofit—it's a lifeline for people who feel lost, broken, and forgotten. "Anchor Point gives so much hope to so many people who might have never seen it any other way," he says with conviction. It's a place where lives are changed, where light shines in the darkest moments, and where second chances turn into new beginnings.

David's story is a testament to the power of purpose and the incredible transformation that happens when we dedicate our lives to helping others. His second chance became a ripple of hope, touching countless lives and proving that even the hardest journeys can lead to the most beautiful destinations.

Avery's Redemption
From Despair to Hope Through the Love of Anchor Point

Avery Williams's story is a deeply emotional journey of despair, resilience, and renewal—a testament to the transformative power of hope and love. At a difficult time in her life, Avery was living through one of the darkest periods she could remember. Pregnant and alone, she had no family to support her, no structure to guide her, and no money to provide for herself or her unborn child. Avery had even pulled away from her church, a place that had once given her strength, leaving her feeling completely isolated. Overwhelmed and broken, she found herself on the verge of giving up—not just on her circumstances, but on life itself.

At her lowest point, Avery felt trapped in a darkness that seemed impossible to escape. The thought of continuing felt unbearable. She wondered if her child would even have a chance if she wasn't around. She thought about ending her life, believing it might be the only way to stop the pain and hopelessness consuming her. But then, something caught her eye—a simple sign that said, "You need help?" In her despair, she couldn't imagine that help was possible, but something stirred within her. She decided to take a chance, walking through the doors of Anchor Point.

Avery's initial visit to Anchor Point was meant to be quick—just a free pregnancy test she desperately needed to apply for Medicaid. She had no expectations, no hope that this would be anything more than a stopgap measure. But what happened next was something she couldn't have anticipated. "The love just poured down on me," she recalls, tears welling in her eyes. From the very first moment, the women at Anchor

Point enveloped her in compassion, care, and encouragement. They saw her not as a failure or a lost cause, but as someone deserving of love and hope.

Avery remembers how they didn't just provide practical help—they gave her the emotional and spiritual support she so desperately needed. "They encouraged me to keep going, to not give up," she says. "When I thought I had no reason to keep trying, they reminded me that I did." The kindness of the Anchor Point team became a lifeline, pulling her out of the darkness and giving her a glimmer of hope when she had none.

In the months that followed, Anchor Point continued to support Avery in ways that transformed her life. They provided essentials like diapers, wipes, and formula—practical items that removed a heavy burden from her shoulders. Avery became an active participant in their programs, completing book reports to earn extra resources for her baby. But the most profound gift they gave her wasn't physical—it was the relentless encouragement to rebuild her faith.

The team at Anchor Point gently encouraged Avery to return to church, something she had been avoiding for years. At first, the idea felt impossible. How could she go back when she felt so broken, so far removed from God? But their persistent love softened her heart, and eventually, she walked back through the doors of a church. That step changed everything. *"I'm so grateful for that,"* she says. "It's made all the difference in my life." Church became not just a place of worship, but a place of healing—a platform for her and her children to start over.

Today, Avery's life is a reflection of the hope and transformation she found through Anchor Point. Her daughter, Ella, is now a vibrant child, lighting up every room she walks into and bringing joy to everyone she meets. Avery herself is thriving. She's nearly finished with her schooling to become a massage therapist, a dream that once felt completely out of reach.

Looking back on where she started, Avery marvels at how far she has come. "There were days I thought I wouldn't survive, but now I see how much life I have to live."

Avery's gratitude for Anchor Point is immeasurable. "To everyone who invests their time, their resources, their love—thank you," she says with a full heart. "You didn't just help me survive. You helped me rebuild my life." She knows firsthand the power of what Anchor Point offers—not just material resources, but the hope, encouragement, and faith that can pull someone back from the edge.

Avery's story is one of darkness turned into light. It's a reminder that even in the most hopeless moments, there is a path forward, and love has the power to change everything. Through Anchor Point, Avery found the courage to keep going, the faith to start over, and the joy of a life she once thought was lost forever.

Anthony's Journey
Finding Connection, Confidence, and Joy in Fatherhood

Anthony's story is one of transformation, hope, and the beauty of finding connection as a father. When he joined Anchor Point's All-Star Dads program, he was looking for a way to connect with other dads who understood the struggles and joys of fatherhood. What he didn't expect was how deeply it would impact his relationship with his son and himself.

Anthony's journey as a dad hadn't always been easy. Growing up without a father, he often felt like he was navigating parenthood without a map. He wanted to be a better dad, to create the bond he longed for but had never experienced. Through All-Star Dads, he found not only the tools to parent more confidently but also the encouragement to create lasting, joyful memories with his son.

One of his favorite moments is when he makes his son laugh. "Even with just a serious look, he starts cracking up like it's the funniest thing in the world," Anthony shares with a smile. "Before, I might have held back, not knowing how to connect. But now, I just grab his little hands, and when he laughs, it feels like pure magic." These small, precious moments have brought them closer, building a bond filled with laughter, trust, and love.

But the impact of All-Star Dads didn't stop there. For Anthony, the coaches became more than mentors—they became like the father figures he never had. "At first, it was just strangers meeting strangers," he admits. "But now, they feel like my dads in a way I never thought possible. They're not just here to do a job. They care. They understand what we're going through, and they genuinely want to help." That support has given Anthony strength and confidence not only as a father but as a man.

Anthony reflects on how the program has changed his life. "If I hadn't found All-Star Dads, I wouldn't be in the positive place I'm in now," he says with emotion. "It's not just about parenting skills. It's about community, growth, and realizing you're not alone." He encourages other dads to join, promising they'll find connection, understanding, and a space to grow. "Don't second-guess it. This is an opportunity to become a better dad, meet other men like you, and create something beautiful for your family."

Anthony's story is a testament to the power of love, laughter, and community. Through All-Star Dads, he has not only strengthened his bond with his son but also found healing for himself. His gratitude is palpable, and his message is clear: "You don't have to do this alone. There's a whole community ready to walk alongside you, and it can change your life, just like it changed mine."

Zoey's Journey
From Fear to Hope Through Anchor Point

After wading through floodwaters from the hurricane, Zoey began to feel unwell. At first, she wondered if it was from the contaminated waters or something else. A pregnancy test revealed the answer—and with it, a wave of overwhelming fear. "I'm pregnant. Now what?"

The news hit her like a storm of its own, leaving her terrified, alone, and consumed by shame. The future felt uncertain, and the weight of it all seemed unbearable. Unsure of where to turn, she poured out her fears to her childhood neighbor, desperately seeking guidance. Her neighbor gently directed her to Anchor Point, telling her, "This is where you need to go." Though hesitant and filled with doubt, Zoey decided to take that first step.

Walking into Anchor Point for the first time, Zoey felt nervous and braced herself for judgment. She expected to be met with harsh looks or cold indifference. Instead, she was greeted with warmth, compassion, and kindness that immediately began to ease her fears. "I felt safe," she recalls, tears in her eyes. Though still afraid, she also felt a glimmer of comfort—a sense that she wasn't alone and that maybe, just maybe, there was hope for her and her baby.

Anchor Point didn't just offer Zoey a place to talk; they surrounded her with resources and support that changed her life. Through educational programs, fellowship, and practical assistance, she began to find her footing. Their baby room, stocked with clothes, toys, diapers, and essentials, was more than just a resource—it was a lifeline. It showed Zoey that she wasn't forgotten, that she and her child mattered. For the first time, she started to feel a spark of excitement about what was to come.

When her son, Kayden, was born, Zoey's heart overflowed. Though he arrived three weeks early, he was a healthy, perfect baby boy. She describes him with awe: "He's an amazing little, tiny, perfect human." Holding him for the first time, she realized that this child, who once filled her with fear, was her greatest blessing—a symbol of light and hope in a life that had felt so dark.

Reflecting on her journey, Zoey recalls a quote that has stayed with her: "Love is the light that sparked when only darkness existed." For her, that light was ignited by Anchor Point. They didn't just provide resources—they embraced her, reminded her of her worth, and showed her that her son was a gift from God. Their love gave her the courage to embrace motherhood and the faith to believe in a brighter future.

Now, Zoey is filled with gratitude and a deep desire to give back. She passionately encourages others to support Anchor Point's mission. "They gave me everything I needed—hope, love, and faith. The least I can do is give back the way they so freely give to others." Her voice trembles with emotion as she says, "Thank you. Thank you for giving me and my son a chance at a beautiful life."

Through her tears, Zoey reflects on one profound truth: *"Anchor Point gave me hope."* Hope in her darkest moment, hope for her son's future, and hope that love and faith can transform even the most overwhelming fear into joy.

A New Beginning
Emilia's Escape to Hope and Safety

Emilia's story is one of courage, resilience, and finding hope through Anchor Point. Trapped in a cycle of abuse, she lived in constant fear for herself and her young son, Noah. Every day felt like walking on eggshells—afraid of saying the wrong thing, cooking the wrong meal, or bringing the wrong drink. The abuse she endured intensified when Noah entered her life, and the fear became unbearable. Her breaking point came on a horrific day when her abuser missed hitting her and struck their son instead. In that devastating moment, Emilia knew she had to escape to protect her child and herself. Desperate for help, she turned to Anchor Point.

Walking into Anchor Point for the first time, Emilia felt a mix of terror and relief. "It was like a weight lifted off my shoulders," she recalls. For the first time in what felt like forever, she experienced safety and warmth. The atmosphere was welcoming, and the staff embraced her with open arms. Emilia finally felt like she wasn't alone. Anchor Point became a sanctuary, a place where she could begin to rebuild her life and heal from the wounds—both seen and unseen—that her abuse had left behind.

Emilia initially struggled to open up about her trauma. Even her parents didn't want to hear the full story, leaving her to carry the pain in silence. But through counseling sessions with Rindy, Emilia found a safe space to speak her truth. "I could finally talk about it," she says, "I could finally feel safe to be who I was meant to be." Each session brought her closer to herself, peeling back the layers of fear and shame, and replacing them with hope and confidence.

Beyond emotional support, Anchor Point provided Emilia with practical resources that made all the difference. Visits to their boutique meant Noah had clothes, toys, and essentials. "It wasn't just stuff," Emilia says, "It was a reminder that someone cared about us." These small acts of kindness began to restore her hope in humanity, helping her believe that a brighter future was possible.

One of the most profound changes came in her relationship with Noah. Before Anchor Point, Emilia found it hard to connect with her son. The constant fear and chaos in their lives had made it difficult to feel the bond she longed for. But as their lives stabilized, their relationship began to bloom. Now, they go to church together, share laughter, and live in the safety and joy Emilia fought so hard to create. Emilia describes the transformation as "hope, awesomeness, and life." Noah, once caught in the shadows of fear, has become a happy, thriving boy.

Emilia reflects on the contrast between their past and present with raw emotion. "We used to cry ourselves to sleep, barricaded in a bedroom, making sure there was no way in. Now, we laugh, we love, we live." She compares Anchor Point to the sturdy center of a bonfire, a foundation that holds everything together. "Jesus is the center of our lives now," she says, her voice filled with gratitude.

Through Anchor Point, Emilia found the strength to escape her abusive relationship, the courage to heal, and the tools to rebuild her life. Her story is one of hope rising from despair, a testament to the power of love, community, and faith. From fear and survival, Emilia and Noah now live in safety, joy, and a future filled with possibilities. Emilia sums it up simply: "Anchor Point didn't just help us escape—they gave us hope."

From Uncertainty to Joy
How Anchor Point Transformed the Elliot Family's Story

The Elliot family's story is one of overwhelming joy, transformation, and discovering faith through the love and support of Anchor Point. When they found out they were expecting their first child, it was a dream come true. They had long hoped for this moment, but alongside the excitement came a flood of fear and uncertainty. Without insurance and unsure where to turn, they faced challenges that felt insurmountable. Anchor Point became their answer—a guiding light in their journey toward parenthood.

Their first ultrasound was a life-changing moment. Seeing their child for the first time made everything real and filled their hearts with awe and gratitude. "It was a blessing—a huge blessing," they recall, their voices trembling with emotion. It wasn't just about the ultrasound—it was about what Anchor Point represented: a community ready to walk with them, support them, and offer hope during a time of uncertainty. From that first appointment, Anchor Point provided more than practical help; they gave the Elliots a foundation of mentorship, fellowship, and love that transformed their lives.

Like many young parents, they wrestled with feelings of being overwhelmed and unprepared. The weight of responsibility felt heavy, and the unknowns of raising a child loomed large. "We were terrified," they admit, "but the kindness and openness of Anchor Point changed everything." The small, caring team showed them that they weren't alone, that they had a community ready to help them navigate this new chapter with confidence. "The amount of care they gave—it shifted our whole mindset about having a child," they share. "What felt like a burden at first became the greatest joy of our lives."

Through Anchor Point's spiritual counseling and mentorship, the Elliots experienced a profound transformation. They describe how they were gently encouraged to reconnect with their faith. "Anchor Point didn't push us or force anything," they say. "They simply showed us that God is here, even in our darkest moments." That realization became a turning point for them, offering a foundation of hope and strength. "The smallest amount of light means everything when you're in the dark," they reflect.

The support they received from Anchor Point was more than just spiritual—it was deeply practical and tangible. The team walked alongside them, ensuring they had the resources, guidance, and encouragement they needed to build a stable foundation for their family. Anchor Point opened doors they didn't even know existed, giving them confidence in their ability to create a safe and loving environment for their child.

Today, the Elliot family looks back with immense gratitude. "They changed our lives," they say. "Anchor Point didn't just help us see our child for the first time—they gave us hope, faith, and the courage to embrace this journey." Their hearts are now filled with joy as they reflect on how far they've come.

Their story is a powerful reminder of how love and compassion can transform fear into confidence and doubt into faith. Through Anchor Point, they found a community that not only supported them but also reminded them of the beauty of God's light, even in life's most challenging moments.

Perfect in His Eyes
Julie's Journey of Healing and Hope

Julie's story is one of heartbreak, resilience, and the extraordinary power of transformation. When she first walked into Anchor Point, she felt like her world was crumbling.

Overwhelmed by pain and shame, Julie carried the weight of emotional wounds that seemed impossible to heal. For so long, she had battled her struggles alone, convinced that no one could understand the depth of her hurt or see her worth. Hope felt like a distant dream, and she believed her brokenness defined her.

As she entered Anchor Point, Julie braced herself for judgment, expecting to be met with pity or indifference. But what happened next shattered her fears. She was met with warmth, kindness, and a love so genuine that it took her breath away. "For the first time in years, I felt seen," Julie recalls, tears in her eyes. "They didn't see me as broken. They saw me as someone worth loving."

Through counseling, Julie began the slow and courageous process of unpacking her pain. Each session became a step toward freedom. At first, it was hard to open up—hard to confront the wounds she had buried so deeply. But her counselor met her with patience and compassion, gently reminding her of a truth she had forgotten: she was not defined by her past. God's love for her was unshakable, and in His eyes, she was already perfect. "Hearing that changed everything," Julie says. "I wasn't a victim—I was a victor. I was God's masterpiece, and nothing could take that away."

There were moments of tears and setbacks, nights when the darkness seemed too overwhelming, and days when doubt crept in. But little by little, Julie began to see herself through a different lens—not as someone broken, but as someone being made whole. She began to believe that her life could be rebuilt, that her story wasn't over, and that God had a purpose for her beyond the pain.

Anchor Point didn't just give Julie emotional support; they gave her practical tools to rebuild her life. Whether through material assistance, fellowship, or educational programs, Julie began to find stability and empowerment. She started to dream again, to imagine a future filled with joy and possibility. "They didn't just help me survive—they helped me thrive," Julie says, her voice filled with hope.

Today, Julie stands as a testament to the power of healing, hope, and God's love. She no longer sees herself as defined by her scars but as someone who overcame. "I look in the mirror now, and I don't see brokenness—I see strength. I see victory. I see someone who is loved beyond measure by God."

Julie's gratitude for Anchor Point overflows. "They didn't just give me support—they gave me back my life. They reminded me that I'm not alone, that I'm worthy, and that I'm perfect in God's eyes." Her journey is proof that even in the darkest valleys, light can break through, and that with love, community, and faith, anything is possible. Julie's story is a powerful reminder that our past doesn't define us—God's love does. Through Anchor Point, she learned to rise above her pain and embrace the truth of who she was created to be: a victor, loved, and perfect in His eyes.

Anchored in Love
Elizabeth's Transformation Through Hope and Support

Elizabeth's story is one of heartbreak, resilience, and discovering the profound power of hope and community. When she found out she was pregnant, she felt the weight of her world collapsing around her. She had just ended a domestic abuse relationship, a chapter of her life marked by fear and pain. Now, facing an unplanned pregnancy and already raising two children—one of whom is autistic—Elizabeth felt overwhelmed, isolated, and lost. The options running through her mind—parenting, adoption, or even abortion—left her in turmoil. She didn't know where to turn for answers or help. Then, through a Facebook group for Texas moms, a stranger mentioned Anchor Point, and her journey toward healing began.

Walking into Anchor Point for the first time, Elizabeth was carrying more than just physical exhaustion—she was weighed down by emotional scars, uncertainty, and a profound sense of hopelessness. "I didn't know what to expect," she recalls, "but I had nowhere else to go." What she found was more than she could have imagined: a community of people ready to embrace her, support her, and guide her toward a future she couldn't yet see for herself. "There are people out there willing to help," Elizabeth realized, and that realization was the first glimmer of light in her darkness.

The moment that changed everything came during her first ultrasound. Watching her baby on the screen, seeing their tiny form and heartbeat, was overwhelming in the best way. "It made it real," she says, her voice thick with emotion. "It changed my mind about so many things." In that moment, Elizabeth's fear began to give way to love, and the weight she had been carrying started to lift.

At Anchor Point, Elizabeth didn't just find practical resources—she found hope, stability, and the courage to move forward. Through the Getting Ready for Baby program, she received diapers, clothing, and even Christmas presents for her children. These small, tangible items felt monumental in her time of need, reminding her that she wasn't alone. Anchor Point also helped her navigate life with her two-year-old son, who had recently been diagnosed with autism. They pointed her toward resources and services she hadn't known existed, giving her the tools to better care for him and, in turn, herself.

More than just material assistance, Anchor Point offered Elizabeth emotional and spiritual support. Counseling sessions became a safe space where she could unpack her pain and begin to heal. Group meetings with other pregnant women who shared similar struggles gave her a sense of belonging and solidarity. "They helped me feel secure and grounded," Elizabeth shares. "For the first time in a long time, I didn't feel so lost."

One of the most profound gifts Elizabeth received was the rekindling of her faith. She describes how Anchor Point gently helped her reconnect with God, not through pressure but through love and encouragement. "They didn't push me back—they helped me find my faith again." That renewed spiritual foundation became her anchor, giving her the strength to imagine a brighter future and the courage to rebuild her life.

Today, Elizabeth is filled with gratitude and hope. Anchor Point helped her realize that she wasn't alone and that she had the strength to overcome her challenges. "Whether you think you're making a small impact or a big impact, you're making a difference," she says with deep emotion. "You've changed my life, and I'll never forget it."

Now, Elizabeth is focused on creating a stable, joyful life for her family. She's exploring ways to further her education and build a future full of opportunities. She looks at her children with pride and sees not just the challenges but the beauty of being their mother. Reflecting on her journey, she says, "I didn't know what I was doing, but Anchor Point showed me that I wasn't alone. They gave me hope, and they reminded me that I can do anything."

Elizabeth's story is a testament to the power of community, compassion, and faith. From a place of heartbreak and fear, she has emerged stronger, filled with the knowledge that she and her children are not just surviving—they are thriving. Her journey reminds us all that even in the darkest moments, hope is always within reach.

Ralinda's Path
Honoring Loss and Embracing Healing at Camp

Ralinda's story is one of healing, growth, and rediscovery. After the profound loss of her son, she made a heartfelt decision to dedicate her time to giving back to others. With her recent retirement, Ralinda felt it was the perfect moment to pour her energy into something meaningful. When she learned about Anchor Point's *Pathway to Hope* camp, she felt called to be part of their mission to support children and families.

Coming to camp was more than just an opportunity to give back—it became a journey of personal reflection and healing. "Camp made me more aware of feelings I've held back for years," Ralinda shares. Growing up, she rarely talked about the hard emotions, focusing instead on the lighter, easier ones. But camp invited her to confront some of those unresolved feelings, helping her reflect on how tragedies in her life, including the loss of her son, had shaped her. "It made me think back to how those moments impacted me, even as a young adult," she says.

Ralinda's experience at camp also gave her the chance to connect with children in a meaningful way, something she hadn't done in a while. She admits she was initially nervous about keeping up with the boundless energy of a younger child but was pleasantly surprised. "It wasn't as exhausting as I thought it would be," she says with a smile. Working with her buddy, Ralinda found joy in encouraging her to explore deeper feelings. "She reminded me of myself—cheerful and upbeat, but holding back the harder emotions." Guiding her buddy to open up about the tougher things was eye-opening for Ralinda, deepening her own understanding of how to approach difficult conversations.

Among the many activities, Ralinda found simple yet powerful lessons in techniques like using band-aids as a way to help children express their internal feelings, not just their external hurts. "The inside hurts are the ones that are hard to talk about," she reflects. "But camp showed me how to gently guide kids toward sharing those feelings." Activities like karate and balloon games brought her closer to her buddy, creating moments of joy and connection.

Reflecting on her time at camp, Ralinda is filled with gratitude. "If you're thinking about helping, I'd encourage you to just jump in," she says. "You don't need to know everything in advance; the leaders guide you every step of the way. It's a good experience for both the kids and for you."

Ralinda sees camp not only as a way to impact children but also as an opportunity for personal growth. "This experience helped me grow, gave me great memories, and reminded me of the importance of relationships—with the kids, the leaders, and the parents." For Ralinda, camp was a healing journey, one that allowed her to honor her son's memory while rediscovering her own strength and compassion. Through her time at camp, she found new ways to connect, to give, and to heal.

Reigniting the Spark
How Camp Restored Angela's Compassion and Joy

Angela's story is one of rediscovery, healing, and the transformative power of giving back. As a teacher with seventeen years of experience, she came to camp worn out, disconnected, and searching for something she couldn't quite name. "I had lost the spark I felt when I first started teaching," she confesses. The compassion and joy that once fueled her seemed to have dimmed, replaced by the weariness of navigating years of challenges in the classroom. Summers were her sanctuary—a time to rest and recover—but when someone invited her to volunteer at Pathway to Hope camp, a tiny part of her was intrigued. Against her initial hesitation, Angela decided to take a leap of faith.

What she found at camp changed everything. Angela expected to learn strategies she could take back to her classroom—ways to better help the children in her low-income school, many of whom had faced significant hardships. What she didn't expect was how deeply camp would impact her on a personal level. "Camp didn't just give me tools for my students," she shares with emotion. "It gave me hope. It reminded me of why I started this journey in the first place."

Working with the children at camp reignited a fire within Angela that she thought she had lost forever. The joy of seeing their resilience and growth, the laughter during activities, and the meaningful conversations about their feelings filled her with a renewed sense of purpose. "Camp helped me find that compassion and empathy I had been missing," she says. "It healed parts of me that I didn't even realize were hurting."

Angela was struck by how camp created a space for both the children and volunteers to grow and heal. As she worked with her buddy, she found herself reflecting on her own struggles and realizing how much she needed this experience. "It's not just about helping the kids," she explains. "It's about learning, growing, and finding hope for yourself, too." Camp reminded Angela that even in the hardest moments, there is always light—always a way forward.

Her favorite part of camp wasn't just seeing the kids smile or discovering strategies to better connect with them. It was the way the experience transformed her own perspective. "I teach music to kids who have been through so much," she explains. "And sometimes, it's hard to see how to reach them, how to help them heal. But camp gave me hope that I can make a difference. It reminded me that even small acts of kindness can change lives."

As she reflects on the experience, Angela is overwhelmed with gratitude. "If I had stayed home this summer, I would've missed something life-changing," she says with tears in her eyes. "Camp filled me in ways I didn't even know I needed. It reminded me that God's plan is always greater than our own, and that when we help others, God helps us, too."

Angela encourages others to take the leap, even if it feels uncertain. "You might think you need rest, but camp will give you something deeper," she says. "It's not just about volunteering—it's about rediscovering yourself, finding hope, and being reminded of the beauty in helping others."

Leaving camp, Angela feels renewed, inspired, and ready to step back into her classroom with a fresh perspective. She carries the lessons, strategies, and hope she gained, knowing that this experience will not only change the lives of the kids she teaches but also her own. "This was more than a camp—it was a gift. A gift of hope, healing, and purpose."

From Struggles to Strength
Naomi and Leilani's Path to Healing

Naomi's story is one of finding hope in the midst of challenges and discovering a path toward healing and connection with her daughter, Leilani. Life before camp was difficult, filled with tension and frustration. Leilani struggled with aggression and defiance, often saying hurtful things because she didn't know how to process her emotions. For Naomi, those moments were heartbreaking. "I could see her pain, but I didn't know how to help her," she says, her voice filled with emotion. Leilani's emotional struggles also manifested physically—frequent complaints of stomachaches, aches, and pains were signs of the turmoil she couldn't articulate. Naomi felt helpless, stuck in a cycle of conflict and misunderstanding.

Coming to camp felt like a leap of faith, but Naomi knew they needed something to break the cycle. What she found was far more than she expected. Watching Leilani work closely with her camp buddy became the most profound part of the experience for Naomi. "The best part was watching Leilani learn," she says, her eyes lighting up with hope. "Her buddy guided her through some really hard work, teaching her how to manage her emotions instead of letting them spiral out of control."

For Naomi, this wasn't just about Leilani learning new tools—it was about seeing her daughter start to believe in herself. "It gave me so much hope," Naomi shares. "For the first time, I saw Leilani beginning to understand her emotions and how to control them. She's learning to express herself in a healthier way, and that changes everything."

Camp didn't just transform Leilani; it also changed Naomi. Through the program, Naomi learned strategies to strengthen her connection with her daughter. She gained insight into how to respond to Leilani's emotional needs and support her in moments of frustration. "This camp didn't just help Leilani," she says with gratitude. "It gave me the tools I needed to parent with more understanding and empathy."

Reflecting on life before camp, Naomi describes the overwhelming feelings of defeat. "It felt like we were stuck, like no matter what I did, I couldn't reach her," she recalls. But now, with the tools and hope she gained, Naomi sees a brighter future ahead. "We have a toolbox now—something we can both pull from to navigate challenges together. I finally feel like we're on the same team."

Naomi encourages other parents who may be hesitant to take the leap and attend camp. "I get it—you have work, obligations, and a million reasons to say no. But trust me, this is the best investment you can make in your child and your relationship with them," she says with conviction. "Camp is life-changing. It's not just about helping your child—it's about healing yourself and growing together as a family."

For Naomi, camp was more than a program—it was a lifeline. It gave her hope, a deeper connection with Leilani, and the confidence to move forward together. She looks to the future with a renewed sense of purpose, knowing they're equipped to face whatever comes their way. "This camp didn't just give us tools," Naomi says through tears. "It gave us hope—and that hope has changed everything."

Building a Future of Hope
The Jones Family's Camp Experience

Frank and Julie Jones' story is one of resilience, healing, and discovering new ways to connect with their daughter, Athena. Adopted from the Democratic Republic of Congo five years ago, ten-year-old Athena came into their lives with challenges rooted in her past experiences. Before attending *Pathway to Hope* camp, life as a family was often turbulent.

The Jones faced significant struggles with Athena's anger outbursts, defiance, and deep emotional pain. *"She would say she hated herself and didn't want to live,"* Julie recalls, her voice heavy with emotion. Instances of aggression and heartbreaking statements made them realize they needed more than just love—they needed help.

Determined to find answers, Julie began researching and came across the camp, which focused on Trust-Based Relational Intervention (TBRI). While they had studied TBRI before, the Jones knew they needed hands-on support to implement it in their family. Camp became their lifeline. "It's one thing to watch videos," Julie explains. "It's another thing entirely to learn how to apply it in real life."

At camp, Athena's emotional challenges came to the surface. In one instance, she tried to knock coffee out of Julie's hand and told her she hated her. But instead of responding with frustration, the tools they learned at camp helped Frank and Julie approach the situation differently. "We didn't get mad. We stepped back and asked her to try again—a redo," Frank says. This new approach allowed them to de-escalate conflicts and create a safe space for Athena to express her emotions without fear.

The Jones describe camp as "absolutely fantastic" for their family. They learned strategies to foster emotional health and connection, not just with Athena but also within themselves as parents. The camp gave them hope that their family could move forward in a healthier, happier way. "We've learned how to help our child be happier and healthier in her emotions," Julie says. "This camp helped us create a safe place for her to come back to, no matter what."

Reflecting on the experience, the Jones are passionate about the importance of supporting programs like Pathway to Hope camp. "There are so many kids out there struggling, so many families falling apart," Frank shares. "This camp brings families back together, gives kids hope, and helps them avoid destructive paths." They emphasize how investing in a program like this creates lasting change: "You're not just helping a child—you're helping a family and building a better society."

For the Jones, the camp didn't just provide tools—it brought healing and hope. Athena is starting to thrive, and their family is stronger and more connected. "Camp showed us how to rebuild trust and love in our family," Julie says. "It's given us a path forward."

Breaking the Silence
Donna's Story of Redemption and Healing

Donna's story is a profound and deeply emotional testimony of transformation—a journey from despair to hope, from condemnation to grace, and from secrecy to forgiveness. For thirty-nine years, Donna carried a secret that she thought would remain hidden forever, a burden so heavy it consumed her. "I expected to take it to my grave," she admits, her voice trembling with the weight of the years she spent in silence. The pain, the guilt, and the condemnation threatened to define her. Yet, God, in His boundless mercy and love, had a different plan for her life.

The moment Donna confessed her burden, everything changed. She experienced the liberating truth of 1 John 1:9: "If we confess our sins, He is faithful and just to forgive us our sins and to cleanse us from all unrighteousness." That confession was a breakthrough—a floodgate of grace that lifted the crushing weight she had carried for nearly four decades. "It restored me," Donna shares, tears of gratitude glistening in her eyes. "It gave me freedom I never thought possible and brought me back to a place of service."

This newfound freedom ignited a purpose within Donna. She turned her pain into a mission to help other women who were trapped in the same despair she had endured. Through Anchor Point, Donna found a way to connect with these women, reaching into their brokenness with the compassion and understanding of someone who had been there. "I know what it's like to feel hopeless, to believe you're beyond forgiveness," she says, her voice filled with empathy. "But I also know what it's like to find grace, healing, and redemption."

Donna and her husband also serve in Anchor Point's sexual abuse recovery group, standing in the gap as surrogate parents for women burdened by the sins of others. This role has been transformative not only for the women they serve but also for Donna herself. "When we ask for forgiveness on behalf of their parents or abusers, it's a powerful moment," she explains. "You can see the weight lifting off their shoulders, the healing beginning to take root." These moments remind Donna of the beauty of God's light shining into the darkest corners of life.

She speaks with awe about the transformations she has witnessed. "They come in broken, hopeless, and filled with despair," Donna says. "But they leave with a sense of purpose, with forgiveness in their hearts, and with hope for the future. Watching that transformation is nothing short of a miracle."

Donna's work has created a ripple effect, with many of the women she has helped now stepping forward to mentor others. This legacy of healing and hope inspires her to continue serving and supporting Anchor Point's mission. "I give because I know what Anchor Point has done for me and for hundreds of women like me," Donna shares, her voice steady but full of emotion. "It's about transforming lives, one by one."

To those carrying secrets, Donna offers a heartfelt plea: "If you're struggling as I did for so long, please don't stay silent. Reach out. Anchor Point is here to offer healing and hope, just as they did for me." She also encourages others to consider supporting Anchor Point's vital work. "Every gift, no matter how small, helps bring light to someone's darkness. You can be part of that transformation."

Donna's story is a powerful reminder that no burden is too heavy for God's grace, no secret too dark for His light. Her journey—from brokenness to wholeness, from despair to purpose—serves as a beacon of hope for countless others. Through confession, forgiveness, and service, Donna has not only found freedom but has become a source of inspiration and healing for so many.

Grace, Renewal, and Twin Blessings
Gabriella's Path to Freedom

Gabriella's story is one of brokenness transformed into beauty, despair turned into redemption, and a life completely renewed by love, faith, and courage. When Gabriella first came to Anchor Point, she carried more than the weight of her circumstances—she carried the pain of a life that felt unworthy of hope. She was emerging from an abusive relationship, grappling with the emotional scars of an abortion just three months prior, and now faced the overwhelming news that she was pregnant again. Already a mother of four children, she didn't know how she could possibly move forward. On the surface, Gabriella seemed to have it all: she owned a thriving business outfitting dancers in clubs across three locations. But beneath the success, her soul was aching, and she longed for something more—a sense of purpose, a light in her darkness.

Her journey toward healing began when she came to Anchor Point. Gabriella was met with open arms, not judgment, and a team of spiritual mentors who saw her worth even when she couldn't. Slowly, they helped her start to rediscover her value as a woman, a mother, and a beloved child of God. "I came in broken and wounded, but for the first time, I felt seen and loved," she recalls.

A pivotal moment came when Gabriella scheduled her first ultrasound at Obrea Medical Clinic. Nervous yet hopeful, she stepped into the room not knowing what to expect. Then the news came—she wasn't just carrying one baby; she was carrying twins. The room filled with emotion as she saw two tiny lives on the screen. Tears streamed down her face as the nurse practitioner lovingly wrote "Hi Mom" in two places on the ultrasound photo.

Gabriella's heart swelled with love and a newfound sense of purpose. "For the first time in a long time, I felt joy," she remembers. Excited, she rushed across the parking lot to the

Hope Family Center, sharing her ultrasound pictures with the staff and volunteers who had become her source of strength.

Through Anchor Point's mentorship, Gabriella's transformation deepened. She began to confront the pain of her past and embrace a future defined not by her mistakes but by her faith. In an act of courage and surrender, she chose to be baptized—pregnant with her twins, standing in her spiritual director's backyard, she made a public commitment to her new life. The waters of baptism symbolized more than a cleansing—it was a rebirth. "It was the moment I realized I was truly free," she says. "Free from shame, free from fear, free to start over."

Determined to leave her old life behind, Gabriella made the bold decision to sell her business and walk away from the world she once knew. But she didn't stop there. Using her experiences as fuel, she launched a ministry to help other women trapped in similar circumstances. Gabriella began visiting clubs, not as a businesswoman but as a mentor, offering Bibles, journals, and resources to women searching for their worth. "I know what it's like to feel lost, and I want these women to know they're not alone," she shares. "They are loved, they are valued, and they can find freedom, too."

Today, Gabriella's life is a testament to transformation. She has remarried, and her twins, Noel and Noah, are living symbols of the beauty that came from her pain. Surrounded by her family, Gabriella reflects on how far she has come. "Those babies saved my life," she says with tears of gratitude. "Anchor Point didn't just give me hope—they gave me a new life."

Gabriella's journey is a powerful example of how Anchor Point's programs change lives. She has become a beacon of hope, reaching out to others with the same love and grace she received. Her story reminds us all of the power of redemption and the profound impact of compassion.

"Together, we are changing the world," Gabriella says with conviction. "One life, sometimes two lives, at a time."

Lena's Light
Finding Grace in the Midst of Despair

Her story is one of heartbreak, desperation, and a journey toward finding light in the darkest of times. As a single mother of three daughters, she had worked tirelessly to rebuild her life after a divorce. She was thriving in her career as a massage therapist, pursuing her dream of becoming a chaplain, and building a future with a wonderful man she was about to marry. Life felt full of promise. But in one horrifying moment, everything she had built came crashing down.

During a massage session, she was assaulted. The trauma left her utterly shattered. Fear, shame, and guilt consumed her as she wrestled with what to do. "If I just stayed silent, maybe it would all go away," she told herself, but the silence felt like it was suffocating her. She couldn't sleep, couldn't eat, and couldn't look at herself in the mirror without feeling disgusted and broken. "I felt worthless," she recalls, "like everything good in my life was slipping away."

Her thoughts turned dark. "What's the point of living?" she asked herself on the loneliest nights, tears streaming down her face. She felt trapped by the overwhelming shame and fear, consumed by the belief that she had lost everything. The despair ran so deep that she began to think that her children might be better off without her. "I thought about ending it all," she admits. "I didn't think I could face another day."

Ten days later, her world was upended again. She found out she was pregnant. This news brought even more fear and confusion. "How could I carry this child?" she asked herself. "How could I explain this? How could I go on?" She confided in a friend, who offered her a way to terminate the pregnancy. Holding the pills in her hand, she stood at the edge of a decision that felt impossible.

I've always been against abortion, she thought, *but maybe this was the only way to survive. Maybe I could erase the pain and move on.* But then another thought broke through the darkness: "What if I hurt my baby? What if I caused her to suffer?" Trembling, she threw the pills to the ground, her tears turning into sobs. "Half of this baby is mine," she realized. "If I can't raise her, someone else will love her. I have to find a way to keep going—for her, for me."

Desperate for help, she turned to Anchor Point. The moment she walked through their doors, she felt something shift. "They didn't judge me," she says, "they loved me." The staff prayed with her, for her, and over her, creating a safe space where she could begin to heal. She joined their sexual abuse recovery program, where she confronted her trauma and found a path forward. "God forgives," she learned. "What happened to me didn't have to define me. My life wasn't over—it was just a new chapter."

Through counseling, she began to see her pain in a new light. She realized she didn't have to hide in the shadows of what had happened. "I couldn't let this stay a dark, horrible secret," she says. "I wanted God to use my story to bring hope to others." She named her daughter Lena Christine, which means "God's shining light." Lena became a symbol of hope and redemption, proof that even the most devastating moments can lead to beauty. "Every time I look at her, I see God's grace in action," she says. "She saved me as much as I saved her."

Her life is now a testimony of resilience and transformation. She opened a women's massage practice, creating a safe and healing environment for others. She continues her studies to become a chaplain, her dream now fueled by a deeper purpose. "I thought I'd lost everything," she reflects, "but God kept it all in place. He took my pain and turned it into something beautiful."

Her gratitude for Anchor Point is immeasurable. "They were my lifeline," she says. "On days when I thought I couldn't go on, they prayed with me and reminded me that I wasn't alone. They gave me hope when I thought there was none left."

Lena Christine's laughter now fills their home, a constant reminder of the strength it took to choose life. "She is my miracle," her mother says, her voice breaking with emotion. "She turned my pain into joy and my despair into hope."

Her story is not just one of survival—it is a story of triumph, of finding beauty in the ashes, and of becoming a beacon of hope for others. "God took my darkest moment and turned it into a testimony," she says. "Lena and I are living proof that there is always light, even in the deepest darkness."

Hands of Love, Hearts of Service
Offering Hope That Changes Everything

We have a deep love and passion for Anchor Point because of the life-affirming, life-supporting, and hope-filled services they provide to so many people in need. Anchor Point meets people where they are, offering everything from adoption support, ultrasounds, parenting classes, and recovery services to counseling and the Obria Medical Clinic. This holistic approach creates a sanctuary for those who are struggling, giving them the tools and support to rebuild their lives. Watching lives transformed through Anchor Point's ministry is a blessing beyond words.

Volunteering at Anchor Point has been a journey of seeing God show up in the most unexpected and beautiful ways. From the moment you step into this community, you feel the presence of something bigger—something holy. The staff and volunteers don't just provide services; they pour their hearts into the clients, creating a ripple effect of love and transformation. Each act of kindness, no matter how small, comes together to form the heart of this ministry. "You don't want to miss seeing how God is at work here," I often tell people.

For me, this journey started with volunteering, but it has grown into so much more. I've been stretched and challenged in ways I never imagined—serving as president of the board and chairperson of the gala, roles that have taken me far out of my comfort zone. Whether it's reaching out to donors, securing auction items, or thanking people for their contributions, these roles have taught me that when God places a passion in your heart, He equips you with the courage to step up and make a difference. It's no longer about what I think I can do, but about what He can do through me.

The stories I've witnessed at Anchor Point are nothing short of miraculous. Parents who felt hopeless now find the strength to rebuild relationships with their children. Women who thought their lives were over discover purpose, healing, and a fresh start. Clients who walked in broken now walk out with hope and a sense of dignity. Every person who serves here—every volunteer, donor, and staff member—plays a role in these transformations.

Anchor Point is more than a place; it is a lifeline. It's a beacon of hope that reminds people they are not alone, that their lives have value, and that their future can be bright again. Hope truly changes everything. It's the reason someone takes that next step, the reason they get up in the morning, the reason they believe in themselves again.

God calls each of us to be His hands and feet, to bring His love to those who are hurting. If you've ever wondered how you can make a difference, Anchor Point is your answer. Whether you give your time, talents, or resources, every contribution helps to offer hope to someone who desperately needs it.

Anchor Point gave me the opportunity to witness lives being rebuilt, families being restored, and hearts being healed. It's a place where miracles happen every day. Hope changes everything, and through Anchor Point, you can be part of changing someone's life. Don't hesitate—say yes to being a part of something so much bigger than yourself. Together, we can bring light to those walking through the darkest valleys and remind them that they are never alone.

Live Color Full
Suzie's Story of Redemption and Renewal

When I was eight years old, a stranger broke into our house in the middle of the night and he sexually abused me. He robbed me of any sense of security that I ever had? He robbed me of a joy that I had in my life that I could never get back.

Sexual abuse leaves wounds so deep that they can feel impossible to heal. For Suzie, it wasn't just her sense of security that was stolen—it was her joy, her creativity, and the unique spark that made her feel alive. "When sexual abuse happens," she says, "it robs you of the things that make you, you." As a child, Suzie had been an award-winning artist, finding joy in vibrant colors and imaginative creations. But after the abuse, she packed away her paints and brushes, burying her love for art beneath layers of pain and loss.

For years, Suzie carried the weight of that brokenness, believing that part of her life was lost forever. But through Anchor Point's support group, she found a glimmer of hope. One evening, their group was asked to pray and ask God what He wanted to restore in their lives. Suzie spent days in prayer, hoping for clarity, but the only answer she received was the word "color." It felt strange and abstract, leaving her puzzled. What could "color" mean for someone like her, whose world had been dulled by trauma?

Weeks later, Suzie sat at her kitchen table with her eight-year-old daughter, who is an artist herself. Her daughter asked her to paint with her, and though hesitant at first, Suzie agreed. As she dipped her brush into the vibrant paints and began to create, a flood of emotions overtook her. "I knew what the word 'color' meant," she says, her voice breaking. "It wasn't just about the paint—it was about bringing back to life the part of me that had been locked away for so long."

In that moment, Suzie felt God's love pouring into her heart, restoring the joy and creativity she thought she had lost forever. "It was as if the floodgates opened," she recalls. Memories of her childhood passion for art came rushing back, and for the first time in years, she felt whole. "What had been lost was restored."

That day marked the beginning of a new chapter for Suzie. She hasn't stopped painting since. Her rediscovered love for art blossomed into a thriving business called Live Colorful. Now, each piece she creates is infused with prayer and hope, a symbol of God's power to heal even the deepest wounds. "Just as God restored my hopes and dreams, I pray He does the same for others through my work," Suzie shares.

Her journey from darkness to light is a powerful reminder that no matter how broken you feel, healing is possible. Suzie encourages others to get involved with Anchor Point, knowing firsthand how their support changes lives. "If you feel a nudge in your heart to serve or give, don't ignore it," she urges. "This is God's way of showing you how to be His hands and feet in your community."

Through God's grace and Anchor Point's unwavering support, Suzie has not only found healing but a renewed purpose. Her life, once shadowed by despair, is now painted with vibrant colors of hope, joy, and faith. And as she prays over each piece of art she creates, she is sharing that light with the world, one brushstroke at a time.

Building Bridges to a Brighter Future at Hope House

Hope House is more than a maternity home; it's a place where shattered lives are mended, dreams are rekindled, and hope is restored. Designed for women sixteen and older facing unplanned pregnancies, Hope House offers a safe haven where they can stay for up to 18 months. During this time, they receive prenatal care, life skills education, and unwavering support to help them transition into independent, thriving lives. Through faith-based guidance and a community of love, these women find the strength to overcome their challenges and embrace a brighter future.

Aaliyah's Story: Turning Pain into Purpose

Aaliyah entered Hope House uncertain and vulnerable. Pregnant and in need of stability, she found more than shelter—she discovered a family. During her ten-month stay, the consistent love and encouragement she received from staff and volunteers made all the difference.

Daily life skills classes taught her essential tools like budgeting and meal planning, while Bible studies provided spiritual nourishment and a sense of peace she hadn't felt in years. The community of mothers and mentors created a sisterhood that lifted her when she felt overwhelmed. "It was like God Himself was embracing me through these people," she shared.

Hope House didn't just meet her immediate needs; it gave her the confidence to dream again. Aaliyah enrolled in nursing school, transitioned into independent living, and recently celebrated the joyous news of her upcoming marriage. Her son, Carter, now has a stable and loving home thanks to the foundation Hope House helped her build.

Serenity's Story: Finding Light in the Darkness

At just eighteen, Serenity faced homelessness while navigating an unplanned pregnancy. With no family support and nowhere to turn, she found herself at Hope House at ten weeks pregnant. Her life, which once felt like a tragedy, began to shift toward hope and possibility.

Through the guidance of Hope House, Serenity was able to stay in school, graduate early, and prepare for her new role as a mother. "It wasn't just a place to live," she said. "It was a place where I learned how to be the mother I wanted to be and build a future for myself and my daughter." Parenting classes and life skills workshops provided her with tools she never thought she'd have.

Today, Serenity's life is a testament to perseverance and grace. She has secured an apartment, a car, and a full-time job while attending school to become a dental hygienist. Her daughter, the light of her life, inspires her every day to keep moving forward.

Lainey's Story: A Path to Reconnection and Redemption

Lainey arrived at Hope House during a difficult season of life. Pregnant with her fourth child, she carried the weight of her circumstances and the fear of what was ahead. But Hope House didn't just provide her with a roof over her head—it gave her a roadmap for healing and rebuilding.

During her stay, Lainey earned her GED with the help of tutoring provided by the program, attended life-changing parenting classes, and found her faith renewed. The relationships she formed with other residents and staff gave her the support she needed to face her challenges head-on.

Her time at Hope House also allowed her to reconnect with her three other children, who had been living in Mississippi.

Now reunited, Lainey is creating a stable and loving home for all her children. As a volunteer at Hope House, she shares her story to inspire other women who feel lost, just as she once did.

The Heart of Hope House

The stories of Aaliyah, Serenity, and Lainey highlight the transformative power of Hope House. Through love, faith, and practical support, this sanctuary turns fear into strength, despair into resilience, and brokenness into beauty. These women didn't just survive—they found the courage to thrive.

Hope House offers more than resources; it offers the gift of hope. With each class, each prayer, and each moment of encouragement, lives are changed forever. For women who feel like there's no way out, Hope House becomes the bridge to a new beginning—a place where they are seen, supported, and reminded of their worth.

If you're considering supporting or volunteering, know this: Your time and generosity make these transformations possible. Together, we can continue to provide hope for women and their children, creating ripples of change that last a lifetime.

A Mother and Son's Journey to Connection and Hope

Camp became a life-changing experience for both Michael and his mother. For her, it was like looking into a mirror and seeing the cracks in her parenting style that she hadn't noticed before. As a single mother to a ten-year-old boy who struggled with emotional outbursts, defiance, and frequent suspensions at school, she often felt defeated and unsure. Her love for Michael was deep, but frustration and exhaustion sometimes led her to react in ways she later regretted. This week of camp, however, offered her a chance to pause, reflect, and embrace a new path forward for their relationship.

One of the most transformative parts of camp for her was observing Michael's buddy interact with him. She watched how the buddy corrected behaviors with love, patience, and consistency, and it inspired her. She began to realize how her own actions and reactions were shaping Michael's behavior. "I need to be the model for the behavior I want to see in my child," she reflected. Through the one-on-one sessions at camp, she gained a deeper understanding of how her lack of structure and occasional moments of giving in were contributing to Michael's struggles. The realization was painful but empowering—she now knew what she needed to change.

For Michael, the transformation was equally remarkable. A boy who had often lashed out or resisted direction, he began to embrace the techniques he learned at camp. He practiced the "bowl of soup" breathing exercise, taking a deep breath to calm down and blowing it out to release frustration. She watched in awe as he even counted his breaths, showing a level of self-control she had never seen before. What once seemed impossible—redoing actions or behaviors—was now something Michael willingly did. Knowing it came from a place of love, not punishment, helped him trust the process.

A moment she will never forget happened during their stay at a hotel for camp. As she struggled with a luggage cart, she asked Michael for help, fully expecting resistance. But instead, he surprised her by walking over, singing "Lean on Me." With a smile, he grabbed the cart and cheerfully said, "I've got it, Mom." She was overwhelmed by the kindness and thoughtfulness of this act—a glimpse into the compassionate and connected child Michael was becoming.

When Michael questioned her about using camp strategies at home, saying, "We're not at camp anymore. Nobody's watching," it gave her the chance to explain a powerful truth. "Michael," she told him, "We didn't come to camp just for a week. We came here to become the best versions of ourselves. These lessons are for our future, and we're going to keep doing hard things together because we can." That conversation solidified their shared commitment to growing together.

The mother also found strength in the community of other parents. Listening to their stories of struggles and triumphs reminded her that she wasn't alone. Each parent's journey was a testament to the power of perseverance and hope. She found herself deeply moved and inspired by their resilience, which gave her the courage to keep moving forward.

Camp didn't just provide tools for managing Michael's behavior—it restored hope and joy to their family. She left camp with a renewed confidence in her ability to parent with love and structure. Michael left with tools to navigate his emotions and a stronger sense of connection with his mom. Together, they stepped into their future not just as a mother and son, but as a team, ready to face challenges with strength, hope, and love.

And through it all, one truth emerged: hope changes everything. Hope is what carried them through the darkness, what gave them the courage to try, and what now lights their way forward.

Debbie Simmons

Twice the Hope
A Mother's Story of Redemption and Transformation

Victoria's story is one of heartbreak, resilience, and transformation through the power of love and faith. After enduring the torment of an abusive relationship, she found herself at a women's shelter, Bay Area Turning Point, desperately trying to piece her life back together. It was there she discovered she was pregnant. Already overwhelmed with caring for her older daughter and struggling financially, the news left her shaken. "How could I possibly do this?" she thought. Her fear and uncertainty grew when an ultrasound at Anchor Point revealed she was not just pregnant—she was carrying twins.

The weight of the news was almost too much to bear. In her darkest moments, Victoria questioned everything. She felt lost, broken, and completely alone. But stepping into Anchor Point, she found something she hadn't felt in a long time: hope. The kindness and compassion of the staff enveloped her like a warm embrace. "It felt like God Himself was saying, 'You're going to be OK,'" she recalls with tears in her eyes. For the first time, she felt seen—not as a victim, but as someone with immense value and potential.

One moment stands out in Victoria's memory: being gifted a purple Bible—her favorite color. "It was beautiful," she says, clutching it tightly. "It became a daily reminder of where I used to be and how far God had brought me." The gift wasn't just an object; it symbolized the love and acceptance she felt at Anchor Point. The staff didn't just offer her help—they offered her friendship, creating a safe space where she could begin to heal.

Through her time at Anchor Point, Victoria found more than support; she found transformation. She began to see herself not as a broken woman defined by her past, but as someone with a future filled with promise. Anchor Point planted seeds of hope in her heart, helping her rebuild her faith and her sense of purpose. "They changed the trajectory of my life," she says with gratitude.

It was during this time that God laid a calling on her heart. Victoria felt compelled to share her journey of healing and redemption. She poured her pain, growth, and triumph into a book titled "A New Woman: The Journey from Pain to Purpose." The book tells the story of how God took her from being a broken girl to becoming the strong, purpose-driven woman she is today. But God didn't stop there. He also inspired her to start a nonprofit organization to support survivors of domestic abuse, ensuring that other women could find the same hope and healing she had experienced.

Reflecting on her time at Anchor Point, Victoria describes it as a place of acceptance, love, and unwavering support. "It wasn't just about helping me—it was about showing me that I was worth helping," she says. The staff prayed with her, believed in her, and encouraged her every step of the way.

Today, Victoria's life is a testament to the power of faith, love, and resilience. Her twins are thriving, her nonprofit is helping others find healing, and her story is inspiring countless women to believe that they, too, can rise from the ashes. "Anchor Point gave me hope when I thought I had none," she says. "It changed my life, and now I can use my story to change the lives of others."

Paris's Journey From Heartache to Hope

Imagine you were a sixteen-year-old girl from a broken home, just finding out you were pregnant. With only your grandmother caring for you, and the added stress of your pregnancy, she decides you need to find somewhere else to live if you parent your baby. Young, alone, and practically homeless, where do you turn? This is exactly the circumstances "Paris" found herself in. She lived with her grandmother because of her family's circumstances, and her grandmother was not happy with her about becoming pregnant due to the extra responsibility of not only raising her granddaughter but having a baby to be responsible for as well. Her grandmother decided it would be best for her to live somewhere else. Can you imagine the heartbreak and pain that Paris went through?

On top of the pain and family struggles, she did not know what to think about becoming a mother. She understood that she was pregnant with a precious baby but found it difficult to think beyond pregnancy and to prepare for what was to come next. One step at a time, Paris began moving forward and received the prenatal care she needed and also found a maternity home as a potential place to live throughout her pregnancy and after her baby was born, instead of with her grandmother. She found Hope House.

Paris moved into Hope House where she could be in a safe environment and receive the support she needs to transition into adulthood and motherhood. There, she attended classes and learned about parenting, labor, cooking, keeping a budget, and so much more. To top it all off Paris was given the opportunity to take courses to prepare her to take the GED test. This was just the place she needed to make the most of her new life as a new momma. She was loved and cared for here but encouraged and given the tools to grow. Her life was changing in the most beautiful way.

Before coming to Hope House, Paris had grown up in a Jehovah's Witness home, but she began growing spiritually as she participated in the bible studies and ended up giving her life over to the Lord. Paris had grown so much and at seven months, she picked a name, and soon would be birthing a beautiful baby that she already loved so much!

Paris now has a healthy, beautiful, baby girl! They are both at Hope House and Paris is in the process of testing and earning her GED. We are so proud of the steps Paris has made and how she has grown and it's because of our community, because of YOU, that she could be a part of Hope House and receive mentorship, education, and the necessary care for her and her baby. That is the impact you made.

Trina's Choice
Finding Hope and Embracing Life

Trina's world felt like it was caving in. A mother of three energetic, beautiful boys, she was already juggling the chaos of motherhood with little support and an overwhelming sense of exhaustion. Then, the news came—she was pregnant again. Instead of joy, she felt a crushing weight of fear and uncertainty. How could she possibly care for another child? The thought of bringing another baby into her already full plate seemed impossible. Torn and devastated, Trina believed abortion was her only option. It wasn't because she didn't love her children or the life growing inside her, but because she loved them so much that she couldn't imagine stretching herself even thinner. She worried her boys would feel neglected if she divided her attention even further.

A small, flickering hope remained deep within her heart. For years, Trina had dreamed of having a baby girl—a daughter to love, nurture, and grow alongside her three boys. But that dream felt unreachable, buried under layers of fear and doubt. She convinced herself there was no way to make it work and began making arrangements to end the pregnancy.

That's when Trina found Hope Family Center. It was a pivotal moment. She met with a compassionate client advocate who listened without judgment and gently guided her to explore all her options. Trina opened up about the deep conflict in her heart—the love she had for her boys, the guilt she felt for even considering abortion, and the tiny sliver of hope she had for the possibility of a baby girl. As they talked, Trina began to see a glimmer of light amidst her darkness. The advocate shared the resources available to her—parenting classes, practical support, and most importantly, a loving community that would walk alongside her.

Then, something unexpected happened. Trina met with a spiritual advocate, who introduced her to the abortion recovery program offered by the center. It was in that conversation that a profound realization hit her like a wave. She thought about the guilt and regret she might face if she went through with an abortion. She understood that while life as a mom of four would be challenging, the thought of taking her baby's life would leave a wound in her heart she couldn't bear. Her tears turned into resolve. If she was going to feel guilt either way, she would choose the guilt she could live with: the guilt of learning to balance the needs of all her children rather than ending her baby's life.

That decision changed everything.

With a renewed sense of hope, Trina moved forward. Soon after, she learned the incredible news—she was carrying the baby girl she had always dreamed of. The moment she saw the ultrasound, joy broke through the fear that had gripped her for weeks. Her precious daughter was on the way, and she knew in her heart that she had made the right choice.

Since then, Trina's life has transformed. Through the resources at Hope Family Center, she has participated in education programs, parenting classes, and Bible studies. She has found a community that uplifts her and helps her navigate the ups and downs of being a mother to four young children. Her boys adore their new baby sister, showering her with love and attention.

Trina's heart is full as she watches her family grow together, bonded by love and resilience. Trina often reflects on how close she came to making a decision that would have left her with heartbreak and regret. She is deeply grateful for the guidance, support, and faithfulness of those who stood beside her during her darkest moments. Through the love and care she received at Hope Family Center, Trina found not only the courage to say "yes" to life but also the tools to build a brighter future for herself and her family.

Today, Trina beams with pride as she cradles her baby girl, her miracle and a reminder of God's faithfulness. Despite the challenges, she knows she is not alone. Her journey is a testament to the power of hope, love, and community, and she continues to inspire others with her strength and determination.

A Journey from Brokenness to Redemption
A Life Renewed Through Hope

She walked into Anchor Point thinking she could help others, but her own story was one of quiet pain and deep scars. Pregnant at nineteen, she made the heartbreaking decision to place her child for adoption. At twenty-one, the weight of fear and uncertainty led her to choose abortion—a decision that haunted her soul. Later, she found joy in marriage and motherhood, welcoming a beautiful son into her life. But even then, loss wasn't done with her. A miscarriage shattered her, leaving her grasping for meaning.

Seeking to channel her grief into purpose, she volunteered at Anchor Point, believing she could pour love and hope into others. Yet, as she stepped into that space of healing, she realized she had wounds of her own that demanded attention. Anchor Point taught her the transformative power of forgiveness—letting go of the chains of anger and shame that bound her to her past. Forgiving her abusers, forgiving herself for her choices—it wasn't easy, but it was freeing.

Life, however, had more trials in store. Her mother's passing sent her into a downward spiral, coping through alcohol and losing the fragile stability she had built. Her marriage unraveled, and she was left feeling utterly alone, with no one to lean on. A year after separating from her husband, she found herself in a new relationship that resulted in an unplanned pregnancy. The weight of fear and hopelessness consumed her as she stood at a crossroads, contemplating abortion.

With her heart breaking and her world spinning out of control, she prayed desperately, "Lord, give me hope." And in that prayer, she thought of Anchor Point—the place where healing began for her years earlier. She called them, her voice trembling, and admitted the depth of her fear and despair.

The response was immediate and filled with grace. The women at Anchor Point embraced her with unconditional love. They didn't judge; they simply held her up when she couldn't stand on her own. Through counseling, resources, and prayer, they spoke life into her broken spirit. Slowly but surely, she began to believe that she wasn't alone, that she had value, and that her story wasn't over.

In one of her sessions at Anchor Point, she found the courage to call her estranged husband. Through tears, she asked him to come home, to rebuild the life they had together, and to raise this child as their own. To her amazement, he didn't hesitate. He returned, bringing with him love and healing, and together they chose to move forward as a family.

Now, her life looks vastly different from those dark days. She sees herself as God does—a beautiful flower pruned by His hand to bloom brightly. Her husband is a devoted father to their daughter, and their family is a testament to the power of grace, forgiveness, and second chances.

"Anchor Point didn't just give me tools; they gave me hope," she shares, her voice thick with emotion. "And that hope saved my life."

Her story is a reminder that even in the darkest valley, there is light. Even when everything feels lost, there is hope—and sometimes, it only takes one brave step to find it.

Partnering to Change Lives
Investing in Hope, Faith, and Legacy

As we close this story of hope, transformation, and eternal impact, we invite you to become part of the ongoing legacy at Anchor Point. Changing lives and building stronger families is not a mission we can accomplish alone. It requires the partnership of compassionate individuals, faithful communities, and visionary supporters who believe in the power of love, faith, and hope to transform the world—one family at a time.

When you partner with Anchor Point, you're doing more than supporting programs and services; you're becoming a vital part of a movement rooted in the promises of God. Every investment, whether financial, through volunteerism, or prayer, becomes a lifeline for families facing life's most difficult storms. Your partnership enables us to offer counseling that restores broken relationships, provides holistic care to women in crisis, and educates parents to build healthier homes. It allows us to point every person we serve to the ultimate source of hope: Jesus Christ.

Imagine being part of a young mother's journey as she discovers that her life has value and purpose. Picture a struggling parent finding the tools to rebuild their family's foundation in love and grace. Envision a teenager rising up as a leader in their community, championing the sanctity of life. These are not distant dreams; they are the stories unfolding every day at Anchor Point because of the faithful support of people like you.

Your investment doesn't just change lives in the present; it creates a ripple effect that reaches into eternity. By partnering with Anchor Point, you are helping leave a legacy that reflects God's faithfulness and transforms generations to come. The hope you give today will echo in the lives of countless families tomorrow, creating a lasting impact that only God can measure.

There are many ways to join this mission:

- **Give Financially:** Your donations empower Anchor Point to expand its reach and sustain its life-changing programs.
- **Volunteer:** Share your time and talents to make a tangible difference in the lives of families.
- **Pray:** Cover our ministry, staff, and the families we serve in prayer, knowing that God moves powerfully through the prayers of His people. Be a part of our 9-1-1 prayer team that intervenes for girls that are struggling with choosing life for their child.
- **Advocate:** Spread the word about Anchor Point's mission and encourage others to get involved.

Get started today at www.AnchorPoint.us. Together, we can make an extraordinary impact, grounded in the truth of Hebrews 6:19a: "We have this hope as an anchor for the soul, firm and secure." This hope—anchored in Christ—is the greatest gift we can offer a hurting world.

We invite you to join us in this sacred work. Together, as partners, we can bring light to darkness, hope to despair, and life to brokenness. Let us invest in something that truly matters: the transformation of lives and the building of a legacy that glorifies God for generations to come.

Thank you for believing in the mission of Anchor Point and for your willingness to make a difference. Together, we are changing lives and shaping eternity.

"Greater love has no one than this: to lay down one's life for one's friends." John 15:13 (NIV)

About the Author

Debbie Simmons: A Faith-Filled Leader Building a Legacy of Impact and Purpose

Debbie Simmons is a woman of unwavering faith, a visionary leader, international speaker, and a legacy builder whose life's work is rooted in her deep trust in God's plan. As the founder and CEO of Anchor Point, a thriving nonprofit dedicated to bringing hope and holistic support to families, Debbie has built an organization that transforms lives both now and for eternity. She is also the author of The Heart of Legacy: Living a Focused, Faithful, and Fearless Life, a book that empowers individuals to live with purpose, courage, and faith.

Married to her husband, Scott, for thirty-four years, Debbie's journey has been one of faith, perseverance, and divine calling. After the heartbreaking loss of their four biological sons, she and Scott turned to God for direction, leading them to adopt nine children and experience the joy of fourteen grandchildren. This journey of loss, love, and redemption has not only shaped Debbie's family but has also fueled her passion for helping others find hope through life's most difficult moments.

Debbie firmly believes that faith is not just a personal conviction but the foundation for every aspect of life—family, business, and leadership. Her ability to trust God in the unknown has guided her as she scaled Anchor Point from a single vision into a thriving enterprise that includes a medical clinic, a maternity home, educational programs, and a range of community services. Through each challenge, she has leaned on God's promises, knowing that every step forward is an act of obedience to His calling.

With an entrepreneurial spirit and a heart for service, Debbie leads with both strategic wisdom and unwavering faith. She has learned that running a nonprofit or a business is not just about making numbers work but about aligning every decision with God's purpose. Whether she is mentoring emerging leaders, making high-level financial decisions, or guiding families through crisis, she remains anchored in the truth that God is the ultimate provider and sustainer.

For Debbie, success is not measured in profits or accolades but in the lives changed through God's grace. She is passionate about inspiring others—whether business or ministry leaders, families , or individuals —to trust in God's plan, take bold steps of faith, and leave behind a legacy that glorifies Him.

Her story is a testament to the power of surrender, resilience, and divine purpose. Debbie continues to challenge and equip others to lead with faith, serve with passion, and build a legacy that echoes in eternity. Whether in the boardroom, at home, or in ministry, her mission is clear: to honor God in all things, trust His timing, and walk fearlessly in the calling He has placed on her life.

Learn more at www.TheDebbieSimmons.com.

Discover more about Anchor Point at www.AnchorPoint.us.

www.ingramcontent.com/pod-product-compliance
Lightning Source LLC
Chambersburg PA
CBHW060833190426
43197CB00039B/2579